HERE
ON THE CHESTER

Washington College Remembers
Old Chestertown

HERE
ON THE CHESTER

Washington College Remembers
Old Chestertown

EDITED BY JOHN LANG

THE LITERARY HOUSE PRESS OF WASHINGTON COLLEGE
CHESTERTOWN, MARYLAND

This project was funded by a grant from
the Donner Foundation.

THE LITERARY HOUSE PRESS OF WASHINGTON COLLEGE
300 Washington Avenue
Chestertown, MD 21620

Printed in the United States of America

Book design by Diane Landskroener
Additional editing by Marcia Landskroener
Vintage photographs from the collection of Tyler Campbell

ISBN 0-937692-18-2

Contents

Foreword

BY HAPPENSTANCE it falls to a new resident of Chestertown to introduce this intriguing collection of reminiscences, impressions, historical vignettes and celebrations, produced by Washington College in commemoration of the 300th anniversary of Chestertown's founding in 2006. Even before I arrived just over a year ago to become the College's twenty-sixth President, I knew that Chestertown was an extraordinary college community. Washington College has defined Chestertown, and Chestertown has defined Washington College. I'm convinced that newcomers and long-time residents alike will enjoy this glimpse of Chestertown through the eyes of people associated with Washington College.

This book, published by the Literary House Press, represents Washington College's tribute to the remarkable community in which we have found ourselves, and an appreciation for the symbiotic relationship we have enjoyed since the College's own founding in 1782. The essays, poems and drawings within these pages, as well as the book's editing and design, are the product of Washington College alumni, staff, professors and students.

In the short time my wife, Sarah, and I have lived here, we have also learned that Chestertown holds its secrets. Oral traditions may pass from generation to generation for decades before seeing print, often gaining depth and color in the passing. We heard early on about a tunnel that connected the house where we live on South Water Street—the Hynson-Ringgold House—with the building now known as the Custom House. Our new neighbors talked with some pride about a Chestertown station on the Underground Railroad. But African-American friends had a less attractive story: that African slaves were brought through that tunnel to be kept in our cellar. Of course we went downstairs to look: no sign of tunnel or slave-quarter remains today. There is no denying, however, that Thomas Ringgold made much of his fortune in the slave trade.

Just as a newcomer stitches a mental quilt of Chestertown by piecing together stories from here and there, readers of this collection will find themselves jumping from descriptions of important landmarks—the Water Tower, the G.A.R. Post, the *Sultana*—to poetic impressions; from famous visitors—George Washington, James Dickey, Little Richard, Ella Fitzgerald—to the reflections of ordinary citizens. Don't miss Trams Hollingsworth's marvelous retelling of her journey with her adopted son Lenox, or Jack Bohrer's chronology of George Washington's many visits to Chestertown. Tea Party Weekend visitors trying to sort fact from fiction will want to read Adam Goodheart's careful examination of the historical record. Rhythm and blues fans: turn immediately to Leslie's Raimond's interview with Pearl Johnson Hackett, Sylvia Hackett Frazier and Rosie Perkins Herbert for priceless information on the legendary artists who performed at the Uptown Club. Enjoy old movies? You'll be delighted to learn of Chestertown's connection to Ginger Rogers and Fred Astaire. Eager to find strong women among the men? Check Marcia Landskroener's celebration of "Women's Work." And there's a sharp dose of reality amidst the nostalgia: African-American Chestertonians get full recognition here, from Elizabeth Clay's fascinating account of black Civil War veterans' creating the Charles Sumner G.A.R. post to the heights and depths and ultimate destruction of the Uptown Club to the visits of Freedom Riders in the 1960s.

So settle down and hone in on the title that seems most intriguing. You may soon find yourself, as I did, reading the volume from cover to cover. Or, you may just pick and choose. Your appreciation for this fascinating town is certain to increase.

Baird Tipson
President, Washington College

Time Capsule

ROY HOOPES

Editor's Note: Roy Hoopes, a journalist and biographer, was director of public relations for Washington College in 1985-86. In 1990, he wrote one of the first—and best—profiles on Chestertown being "discovered." Some of the people named here have moved to other positions, and some are deceased. Some of the businesses mentioned are no more. Readers will be amused to note that realtors were marveling, then, how a townhouse near the waterfront had sold for $210,000. Yet the insights here into the character of Chestertown are as true today as they were when this story first appeared in Maryland Magazine.

RENOWNED EDITOR AND ESSAYIST Bernard DeVoto once said that the ideal retirement town must have a good hospital and a college. To these prerequisites for the ideal place to live or retire, one may add other requirements: a lively local paper; a newsstand where you can buy *The New York Times* and the best weekly, monthly and quarterly magazines; cable TV; a major body of water nearby; and finally—most important—a population of interesting people, which, more often than not, is provided by a college, one way or another.

Put them all together and you have what some think is the best little town on the eastern seaboard—Chestertown.

For years, the residents of this often-called "jewel-like town" would urge reporters from nearby metropolitan areas to keep it "our little secret." But no more. Alas, Chestertown and its surrounding farmlands have been discovered by retirees, weekenders and tourists from Washington, Baltimore, Wilmington, Philadelphia, Pittsburgh and Florida. Waterfront property in or near town has been virtually impossible to find at reasonable prices for three or four years and in-town houses come on the market very rarely. What happened to Easton, Cambridge and Oxford a few years ago is happening here.

The only question is: What took it so long? A couple of years ago, *The Atlantic Monthly* reported that more and more designers have discovered the essence of the perfect community. "The newest idea in planning," said Andres Duany, co-planner of the highly acclaimed Seaside, Florida, "is the 19th-century town. That's what's really selling."

If 19th-century towns are the model now, Chestertown, as an 18th-century town—and a major one at that—should have been discovered long ago. But the reason for its prolonged obscurity is that from the late 18th century, when the post roads began following the Western Shore, to the early 19th-century emergence of Baltimore as the most important port in Maryland, Chestertown just sort of got lost. For 200 years, as Robert Brugger put it in his history, *Maryland, A Middle Temperament: 1634-1980*, the Eastern Shore towns of Easton, Cambridge and Chestertown "nestled themselves in the ways of the past."

Often a town's true character is established by its past and Chestertown's historical credentials are impressive. It was laid out in 1706 as the Kent County seat and known as "New Town," but gradually its proximity to the Chester River established its name.

By the Revolution, Chestertown at the height of its colonial prosperity was, next to Annapolis, the most important port in the State. It was also along the route from Philadelphia to Richmond, and travelers, including George Washington who made the trip many times, would cross on the ferry from nearby Rock Hall to Annapolis.

Chestertown also had its own anti-British Tea Party—when citizens threw bales of tea off the *Geddes*. In 1781, when Washington's aide, Tench Tilghman, made his famous ride from Yorktown to Philadelphia to inform the Continental Congress that Cornwallis had surrendered, he passed through Chestertown. The following year, Rev. William Smith, who many believe to be the founding father of education in the new world, founded Washington College with the encouragement and financial support of its namesake.

But then, the focus began to shift to the Western Shore. The cost of shipping freight was much cheaper by sea than by land, and Baltimore, which was closer than Philadelphia, Boston and New York to the emerging markets in the Midwest, became the preferable port. Moreover, it became even more attractive in the 19th century with the building of the Baltimore and Ohio Railroad. It was then that Chestertown began its 200-year slumber.

"We have pursued a bucolic, mellow kind of existence since the Revolution," said Hurtt Deringer, [deceased] editor of *The Kent County News* (itself an integral part of the town's past, having been launched in 1793 as *The Chestertown Spy*). "We have gone our way—hardheaded, stubborn and insulated from the rest of the world."

This insulation was perhaps a good thing. With nothing much happening for most of two centuries, there were not many changes made, which means that when the town planners started discovering the virtues of 19th-century towns and building new ones to look like them, lo and behold, here was the real article virtually intact with its custom house, historic little college, and many 18th-century houses nestled quietly on the banks of the Chester River.

"The 19th-century towns are completely viable prototypes," says town planner Duany. "But it's not enough to look like a town—it has to function like a town," which means that it must be able to govern itself flexibly and in the democratic tradition. Chestertown is governed by a "strong mayor," meaning he [now she] has a vote in the Town Council, and four ward council members elected on staggered four-year terms, as is the mayor. . . .But it is actually run by a permanent town manager, Bill Ingersoll. "I'm like an executive officer," he says. "I carry out orders from the mayor and follow policies set by the town council."

However, it is not enough to look like a town, function like one, or even be nestled in one of the most ideal locations on the eastern seaboard. There has to be something else, and there is, because Chestertown today is booming. "When the weather is good," says Margo Bailey, proprietor of the Chestertown Newsstand [and now the mayor], "we get as many as four or five tourist families a day in here inquiring about real estate offices and housing in the area." Hurst Purnell, a local real estate broker, concurs. "There is virtually no property left on the water, and a townhouse just up from the Custom House sold not long ago for $210,000."

Almost anyone you talk to will tell you that the reason Chestertown is booming—and, more important, attracting interesting people—is the presence of Washington College. "What the college brings to the town is a sense of culture—foreign flicks, Edward Albee giving a lecture, the Julliard String Quartet," says Bob Day, who teaches creative writing at the college. The college also has a way of bringing out the best in people, like the late Bob Forney who ran a jewelry store but was also the force behind the college community concert series.

The college makes available to the local citizens its swimming pool, gymnasium, tennis courts, and library in addition to presenting a wide variety of lectures, concerts, musicals, special films, plays and poetry readings. Moreover, it offers an extensive program of adult education courses to people who come from all around Chestertown to take classes.

"I can't imagine living in Chestertown without the college," says Marsha Fritz, an architect who chose Chestertown as the place to hang out her shingle. "There is something to do every night at the college, if you want to go." And a young man who was installing a new propane heater in the Water Street home of one of the college deans told the dean, "I can't tell you how much the college being in this town means to me. I go to all the lectures and exhibits and basketball games."

Is it also any wonder that Chestertown has become especially attractive to seniors looking for a place to retire? Today, an estimated 29 percent of its residents are over 60 (compared to 20 percent in 1970) and, of course, they are especially appreciative of Bernard DeVoto's other prerequisite—a good hospital. The Kent and Queen Anne's Hospital is highly valued and avidly supported by all its citizens, old and young alike. A recent walkathon raised more than $1,300 for a new room in the intensive care unit.

So today the bucolic little 18th-century town nestled on the Chester River, just over ten miles from the mouth of the Chesapeake Bay, has become a stimulating intellectual and cultural center, primarily as a result of two very dissimilar catalysts—the bridge, and more recently, Douglass Cater.

When the Chesapeake Bay Bridge came in 1952, it had no immediate impact on Chestertown, which was mostly ignored by the stream of automobiles heading for the ocean. Having waited 100 years or so for quick transportation to the Atlantic, who cared about the Chester River? A few seekers of the good life took the opportunity afforded by the new bridge to establish beachheads in Cambridge, Easton and Oxford. But very few took the time or effort to explore shunpike 213 north beyond Centreville into the rurals or on to Kent County unless they were headed for Washington College.

The bridge, however, did have an impact on the college. As the late Elizabeth Sutton Duvall, a 1930 graduate of what is certifiably the tenth and arguably the fifth oldest college in the country, recalls, before the bridge, most of the speakers and performers at the school were from the Eastern Shore. But after the bridge, special events planners were able to bring nationally known personalities to the college. By the 1960s, the William James Forum (founded by philosophy professor Peter Tapke) and the Sophie Kerr Lectures . . . were bringing a continuing parade of distinguished philosophers, scientists, historians, dramatists, poets and novelists to lecture at the college.

The forum brings one speaker a month during the school year to campus, men and women of broad experience, achievers in their field who are often controversial. They have included Mortimer Adler, Betty Friedan, and Senators Paul Sarbanes, Joseph Biden and Charles Mathias. "The forum is a feast of enlightenment that people pay nothing for," says Tapke. And the charm of Chestertown plays no small part in attracting distinguished speakers to the campus. "People love to come here," adds Tapke. "Washington College is only 90 minutes from the

Beltway and Bill Colby (former CIA Director] liked to sail his boat to Chestertown."

Music is another cultural ingredient the college brings to the town in large doses. The Music Department, under professor Garry Clarke, stages a succession of concerts, solo performances, musicals and an annual Renaissance Dinner complete with music.

The college is aware that the townspeople attend these concerts and considers them an important part of the audience. "The concert series committee is made up of faculty, students and townspeople," says Clarke, "and although we put the emphasis on educational choices for our music, we think the townspeople are a wonderful and important part of our audience. When we put on the Renaissance dinners, people come not only from Chestertown, but Washington, Wilmington and Dover."

Similarly, the English Department is aware of local interest in the writers it recruits. The framed posters on the walls of the college's Rose O'Neill Literary House provide a sampling of the writing talent brought to Chestertown by a contribution from the well-known Eastern Shore writer, Sophie Kerr. Half of the interest from her significant donation pays for the lecture series, the other half for what is easily the most attractive undergraduate literary award in the world—up to $30,000 (depending on the interest rate that year) to the most promising senior writer. Sophie Kerr lecturers have included poet laureate Richard Wilbur, James Dickey, John Barth, Katherine Anne Porter, Steven Spender, Paul Horgan, Brendan Gill, Edward Albee, Toni Morrison, Robert L. Helibrone, Joseph Brodsky, Angus Wilson, William Styron, Mary Lee Settle, Susan Minot and Alan Ginsburg.

And then, in 1982, came Douglass Cater, as new president of Washington College. Cater was something of an Establishment dynamo with years of experience in the corridors of power as Washington Bureau Chief for the old *Reporter* magazine, special education assistant in Lyndon Johnson's White House, a director of the Aspen Institute, publisher of *The London Observer*, author of several highly praised books on journalism and government, and even a novel (*Dana*).

He was also known to have a short fuse and more than a touch of Dean Acheson abrasiveness. As one journalist who knew Cater from his *Reporter* days said, "I always wondered how Doug would fare in the world of small college academics, rich Republicans, and teenagers"—three groups that any college president must deal with regularly.

But despite—or perhaps because of—his sometimes Olympian manner, most everyone inside and outside the college agrees that he fared brilliantly in his eight-year tenure. At dinner, faculty members sometimes toast Cater "as the man who brought urban tensions to the Eastern Shore." However, one professor stated, "No matter how you feel about Cater personally, I think we all agree that he has had a tremendous impact on the college."

"Cater had a higher profile than the college when he arrived," says Dave Wheelan, the college's development officer, "and his continual op ed articles in *The New York Times, Washington Post and Baltimore Sun* have helped keep the focus on the college—and the town." In fact, it was Douglass Cater who took on then-Secretary of Education William Bennett in a memorable debate—conducted on the op ed pages of the major dailies—on the question of whether higher education was or was not too greedy in its quest for funds.

Cater's own quest for funds was eminently successful. With the help of his two fund-raising chairmen—Alonzo Decker, Jr., and W. James Price IV—enough money has been raised to totally revamp the appearance, as well as the efficiency, of the campus. And Cater's personal intellectual network helped bring, through his President's Forum, convocation speakers and the Woodrow Wilson Fellows, still another regiment of distinguished speakers—again accessible to Chestertonians: David Brinkley, Roger Mudd, Bill Moyers, Lady Bird Johnson, the Honorable Sandra Day O'Connor, Senator Edmund Muskie, Robert MacNeil, Mark Russell, Art Buchwald, Walter Cronkite, Meg Greenfield and many, many more.

Inevitably this intellectual and cultural inclusion into a community that was virtually cut off from the mainstream for nearly 200 years had its impact. The result has been to bring to the shores of the Chester a variety of interesting people attracted to and eventually, in one way or another, associated with the college. Take George and Jane Dean, for example. Dean, a lawyer, had spent most of his life trying civil rights cases in

Montgomery, Alabama, before suddenly coming into big money by representing one of the heirs of the legendary Howard Hughes. Even before the estate was settled, the Deans had enough money to enable them to live anywhere they wanted. They chose Chestertown for a number of reasons. One was its location: Dean was once an avid hunter and had shot some geese in the Chestertown area. But there was another factor: Dean had known Douglass Cater in Montgomery, where they both grew up. About the time Dean was considering a move to Chestertown, he heard that Cater was soon to be appointed president of Washington College. "We knew Cater had both feet planted in the 20th century," says Dean, "and he might even bring a little Potomac fever to the Chester."

So the Deans moved to Chestertown where they became active not only in historical preservation (restoring among other buildings what surely must be the finest little Victorian hotel in colonial America, the Imperial on High Street), but also in the college. There he helped establish a scholarship fund for African-American students, worked with The 1782 Society and other college fundraising activities, and made a substantial financial contribution to the college.

Then there was Constance Stuart Larrabee, a world-class photographer whose work was included in Edward Steichen's "Family of Man" exhibit and book. For years she and her husband, Sterling Larrabee, lived on a 30-acre farm near Chestertown where they developed ties with the college. After her husband died, she moved into town and was soon very involved with the college—as founder of the Washington College Friends of the Arts and principal fundraiser for and contributor to the college's Creative Arts Center, which was named for her.

Katherine Orme, a divorcée from Easton who came to Chestertown to go back to school, was struck by how quickly she got "to be known in the small shops, the genuinely friendly atmosphere and acceptance by some of the older townspeople, and the variety of life in a college town." But she had some trepidation. "It was clear that another single woman was not what the town needed. It already had a shortage of men" (which she added to by marrying one of her college professors).

Or, take Davy McCall, a former World Bank and State Department economist, whose hobby is historic architecture. In 1984, he retired to his farm at Rock Hall and started teaching part-time at the college. Eventually he became chairman of the Economics Department and became so caught up in college that he felt compelled to move to Chestertown where he remodeled an old house.

Dr. Theodore Kurze [now deceased] was a college alumnus and retired neurosurgeon who, in 1957, pioneered brain surgery through a microscope. Cater lured him back to Chestertown to teach a course in medical ethics—and enjoy life in a college town. "My entire life has been spent in academic circles," said Kurze. "But I'm a sufficiently Dionysian person, so unless I am stimulated by the world of ideas I tend to go into default drive."

As the experiences of these people suggest, if Washington College is the engine that drives this little cultural enclave on the Chester River, the key to getting the most out of life in this town is involvement—in one way or another—with the college. One way, of course, is through the Development Office if one cares to make a contribution. But there are many other ways—as a friend of the arts, a volunteer worker in numerous campus and civic projects, a part-time teacher, a student in the adult education programs, etc.

[Then] Mayor Elmer Horsey agreed that the college plays a critical role in his town. "About twelve years ago (during the administration of Joseph McLain) our relations with the college began to improve," says Horsey, "and today under President Cater, we have a wonderful relationship." And Cater says, "In a town as small as this and a college as small as this, it is essential that you give some thought and attention to the town and gown relationship."

There have been some problems with students living off campus during the recent college construction program, but "they're learning now that they have to live by the town rules," said Horsey. Students living in group housing have also made it difficult for local working people to find affordable rentals in town; one real estate broker spoke of at least twenty-five parents of children attending college buying houses, which their children live in (with other students paying rent) while they are in school.

Despite the impact of the 800 college students and nearly 200 faculty and staff on Chestertown's approximately 4,000 citizens, "it is not a company town," one professor stresses. It has, through the changes, retained its historic tradition, which adds to its charms. For instance, there are "the old Tories who say they wished England had never lost the war and mean it," says the professor. The town has also remained insulated. As the story goes, there was a woman from Baltimore who came to Chestertown at the age of two, and when she died, the Kent County paper reported, "Baltimore Woman Dies at 92." Editor Deringer says, "The woman really lived in Centreville a few miles away, but everyone thinks it could have happened here, although I would never have headlined it that way in my paper."

But Chestertown is not a museum. The phrase you hear often to describe it is "a lived-in Williamsburg." Robert Janson-LaPalme, professor of art at the college and eleven-year chairman of Chestertown's Historic District Commission, says, "There are more 18th-century buildings and foundations in Chestertown than in any other Maryland town except Annapolis." And LaPalme is determined to see that Chestertown remains as much as it can an 18th-century town. "We are trying to retain the integrity of the original structures," he says, "but at the same time make them livable in the 20th century. And we are interested not just in the mansions—which are great—but also the modest dwellings."

And don't forget the Chestertown Newsstand with its nearly fifty-foot magazine rack full of every magazine you can imagine, from *The Atlantic Monthly* to *Soldier of Fortune* and *Model Railroads*. "People in a college town have eclectic tastes," says Margo Bailey, whose husband and co-owner of the newsstand, Mike Bailey, teaches economics at the college. All of which helps make the newsstand the "gossip center" of town, as all good newsstands are—the place where you gather around the register for a cup of coffee in the morning, the place which helps outlanders know where they really live. "For people on the nearby farms," says one Chestertonian, "your town is where you buy your Sunday paper." One such Sunday customer is novelist John Barth, who has a place a few miles outside of town and occasionally gives readings at the college.

So, people come from miles around to Chestertown to buy Sunday papers, attend lectures, listen to music, look at paintings, photographs and films, and use the college athletic facilities. Many settle down to live here. Perhaps it is because they have become so fed up with urban life that they identify with the local story of Peter Parker, a British officer during the Revolutionary War, who reportedly said on the eve of a local battle: "I will have breakfast in Chestertown—or in Hell."

Chestertown may not be heaven—but a lot of people living in the little college town think it may be the next best thing.

No Title At All

JIM LANDSKROENER

AUTHOR'S DISCLAIMER:

In the preface to one of his novels, Mark Twain stated, "No weather will be found in this book." He went on to note that, "Nothing breaks up an author's progress like having to stop every few pages to fuss-up the weather," and also, "Weather is a literary specialty, and no untrained hand can turn out a good article of it." Furthermore, said Twain of himself, "The present author can do only a few trifling ordinary kinds of weather, and he cannot do those very good. So it has seemed wisest to borrow such weather as is necessary for the book from qualified and recognized experts—giving credit of course. This weather will be found over in the back part of the book, out of the way. See Appendix. The reader is requested to turn over and help himself from time to time as he goes along."

Now here we are, only one paragraph into it, and you are probably thinking, "huh?" Let me explain. It was my understanding that the short narrative you have now encountered, perhaps unwittingly, was intended to be a remembrance of Chestertown. Because I have lived here, since birth, some fifty years now, I am quite intimate with Chestertown and its environs and was more than agreeable to putting my memories to paper. However, fifty years is a long time, and quite frankly, my grasp of precise names, dates, locations and all other "facts" is somewhat tenuous, if that's the right word. Thus this disclaimer. I decided not to let this lack of precision discourage or slow me down. To borrow another bit of Twain's seemingly infinite wisdom, "Never let the truth get in the way of a good story." So, like Mr. Twain and his weather, I will leave the elucidation of facts to "qualified and recognized experts." I'll use the shorthand "see appendix" {which will not be found} whenever I think I might be on a slippery slope. Okay? Good, then let's proceed with…

THE TITLE

Since I'm past my deadline, I have a feeling that most of the good titles have probably been taken already. You know, like "Chestertown, A Remembrance," or "Chestertown, A Quaint and Cozy Armchair of a Town," or "The Gentle Hand of Colonial Charm—How To Do It Right!" or even "A Study of Brick Sidewalks."

So I am going to suggest something radical at this point, no title at all! Brilliant. No preconceived notions on your part, it will take the pressure off me, and leave open the chance that something will occur to me later. Great, so let's jump right into it, shall we?

THE FIFTIES

I was born at Chestertown hospital in 1954, delivered unto this world by Dr. A. C. Dick, a man way up there on my "favorite people of all time list" and a true character. He had the best face, big gentle eyes and great smile. He stitched me up whenever I cut myself badly (once every two years it seems), and he loved giving my mother a hard time about it whenever she had to take me in there, as if it were her fault. Even when he was old and his hands were a little shaky, I didn't want anyone coming at me with a suture unless it was Dr. Dick. He drove this beat-up old green VW bug everywhere at forty miles an hour. In town, out in the country, across the A & P parking lot, it didn't matter—forty miles an hour.

But I digress. Looking back, I think the decade we sometimes refer to reverently as "the Fifties" started when I was born and lasted for the next ten years, right up to JFK's assassination. It was a time when phones had no dials or buttons; you just picked it up and told the lady on the other end who it was that you wanted to call. It was a time when there were only three TV stations, black and white of course, and cartoons could only be found on Saturday mornings. During that time, I saw Chestertown as consisting of three places: Stam's Drug Store, the Chester Theater and Otis's Barbershop.

The soda fountain at Stam's Drug Store, which due to some weird space-time continuum thing has not aged since it was brought over by Captain John Smith, was the domain of one Miss Harriet. Unless you knew her well, you would think that Miss Harriet suffered some odd affliction which made it impossible for her to smile. Not that her face was expressionless. She had at least ten variations of scowl, four or five of indifference, and every now and then threw in the odd silent reproach, but only when the occasion called for it so as not to overuse what was, in the timid heart of a six-year-old, a very powerful and significant form of communication. Nonetheless, I harbored a certain cautious fondness for Miss Harriet. She clearly liked my mother and was always nice to me—I nurtured the notion that she always gave me just a little extra squirt of vanilla in my vanilla Cokes. And if I was ever stuck in town (we lived out Quaker Neck Road) and needed to call home, she would let me use the pay phone at the back of the store for free.

The Chester Theater was great, because it was the only other source of cartoons, and it was the only place where it was socially acceptable to eat your brains out on candy. I was always so impressed by the short ad reel that preceded every show. There, up on the silver screen, were actual ads for local businesses! It was all so. . . amazing. Chestertown Bank had one, though if you wanted to see the real thing all you had to do was leave the theater to see that imposing gray edifice in all its jerky, streaky magnificence. It was absolutely breathtaking. I never tired of it. Then, there was Otis's Barbershop. It was on High Street just a few doors up from what is now Andy's. Otis's was a little walk-down, I guess that's what you'd call it, below street level. There were three chairs but I seem to remember there being only two barbers—Otis, who never cut my hair, and Eddie Lane. Eddie was my man. He was what my mother might have referred to as a real Dapper Dan. Thin as a rail and perfectly coifed in a gray flattop and pencil thin, salt and pepper mustache, Eddie looked like he lived the meaning of a "sharp-dressed man." Otis's was a cool little world all unto its own. Comic books, oh man there were comic books!

Eddie was a smoker, Lucky's or Camels or one of those non-filtered, man's man cigarettes. He didn't use an ashtray, just hung the lit end over the counter. I used to love blowing softly on the lit end just to see it glow, savoring the smell, and feeling somehow useful in my vigilance by not letting it go out as he worked on my brother Chris's head.

To this day, I love the smell of cigarette smoke as it comes lazily off the lit end.

THE SIXTIES

This decade began, as far as I'm concerned, with the arrival of the Beatles and ended ten years later with the departure of Richard Nixon. This span of time, tumultuous for the country to say the least, also neatly coincided with my own journey through the craziness of adolescence and teenager-hood.

My Sixties decade began at the Chestertown bowling alley. Yes Gracie, Chestertown had its own bowling alley. It was down on Cannon Street, next to the Hynson-Ringgold House. I seem to remember there being four lanes, strictly duckpins, though on this specific point I suggest you see appendix. I was there for a birthday party. It was a long, narrow place and as you walked in there was a counter on the right for food, drinks and shoes, I suppose, to the left a few tables and the alleys toward the back. This was probably not the first time I had been in there, but it was the first time I can remember paying attention to that icon of American culture—the jukebox.

The girls started pumping it full of nickels, and the first song out was a Beatles number. At this point in time, "I Want to Hold Your Hand" had been the number one song forever. Mary Ellen Simpkins, a girl in my neighborhood, had one of those little record players that closed up like a typewriter case. You know the kind, two latches and a handle in the front and a cheesy little speaker in the top. Anyway, I had heard lots of Beatles coming out of that record player and really only paid attention because the girls seemed to think it was so important.

But that day in the bowling alley, the first song out was "I Saw Her Standing There," the B side of "I Want to Hold Your Hand." Somehow, the jukebox was turned way up, and I heard for the first time in my life true rock and roll, loud. Glorious bass beating against your chest loud, the way God intended it loud, grabbing your timid little white boy soul by the behind and shaken' it baby shaken' it loud. Sorry parents, but nothing in life can prepare a kid for his first experience with loud rock and roll.

Unfortunately, this was probably the highlight of the decade for me. Kids, forget the Madison Avenue and Hollywood spin you've been fed about the Sixties for all these years. The Sixties were not an idyllic, peace-love, hippie-dippy joyfest. The Sixties were mean, man. The world suddenly split into rival gangs: young vs. old, black vs. white, rich vs. poor, Republicans vs. everybody, hippies vs. rednecks. People that you had known and admired all your life were suddenly angry, suspicious and threatening. No place was safe, and for the next ten years I decided to take the "middle child" approach to life. Keep my head down, my eyes open, and always know the location of the nearest exit.

Rumors that the Freedom Riders might try to pass through town spawned other rumors that camo-wearing, shotgun-toting citizens of the Right would be there to meet the buses with good ol' Eastern Shore, 12-gauge hospitality.

And those crazy college kids up on the hill were doing what most crazy college kids throughout the country were doing in the late 1960s, protesting the war. The locals were not all that thrilled about it either. When I was twelve or thirteen, there had just been a protest march. I was in Stam's and this nice old man, someone I had known, trusted and admired all my life, came up to me as I stood at the counter and gently put his hands on both my shoulders, looked me in the eye and said, "What do you think of all this protest nonsense?"

Well, I'm nobody's fool, and the phrasing of the question clearly did not invite free and sociable discourse on the matter. So I stayed quiet and gave him my best "Why whatever do you mean, sir?" look. After a lingering pause, he said, "I just wanted to know whether I should do this," tapping my shoulders gently with his big hands, "or This." Then he put his hands around my neck and gave a little squeeze for emphasis. Scared the you-know-what out of me.

That, in a single instant, was the Sixties for me and almost everybody else. Everything was the same and everything was different and out there somewhere people you knew or didn't know maybe hated your guts. For ten years, the life of an adolescent in a small country town as handed down to us from Twain to Gilbert Byron disappeared. Tom Sawyer morphed into Holden Caufield, and by the time it was all over, even the President of the United States was keeping his head down and looking for an exit.

THE SEVENTIES

My Seventies began with Gerald Ford and his insipid WIN buttons (Whip Inflation Now!) and ended when the Clash gave us "London Calling" (1980), an album that finally drove the broken neck of a guitar through the heart of disco. That makes it a really short decade, maybe six years tops. But I think that's all the Seventies deserved anyway.

I was finished with college and living on High Street at the time. Right down the street from my apartment was a second-hand furniture store, long gone now. When I moved in, I bought a sofa for ten bucks, a dresser for twenty-five and a kitchen table and chairs for fifteen. I went to Ames and spent ten bucks on dishes and another fifteen on "silverware."

So my apartment was a little shabby, so what. Chestertown had become a little shabby, too. The economy stunk, gas was now twice as expensive, hell everything (except for fourth-hand furniture) was now twice as expensive. But that was okay. I had mined the town for lumps of fool's gold, and found that it was good.

My fondest memory of those dingy years was the Chestertown Tea Party. I think someone, probably Jack Schroeder, realized that we needed a good excuse for a party with a capital P. In the beginning, these were not the huge affairs they have become. For the most part you got a moderate dose of "colonial" amusement in the form of the reenactments of various sorts, a chance to buy a few cheesy, colonial-type souvenirs, and your fill of fried clams and funnel cake.

In those first several years, this event was not much of a tourist attraction. It was a chance to see old friends whom you rarely ran into the rest of the year. Did I mention you could drink beer? On the street? With all those around you encouraging this unique (at the time, anyway) malty conviviality?

The Chestertown Tea Party revived the town in a way no other event could have possibly done. It brought life and friendship and community out into the open again. With fried clams.

True, the Tea Party these days is more of a crowded spectacle than most of us would like. And the weekend seems to exist for the benefit of those weary vendors who travel from festival to festival. And it takes half an hour to buy anything to eat or drink. So be it; I wouldn't miss it for the world. I can still stand in the middle of the intersection of High and Cross Streets, a beer in one hand and a cup of fried clams in the other, look up the street toward my old apartment, and consider myself home.

THE EIGHTIES

The Eighties was the decade when we baby boomers were either into or rapidly closing in on our thirties, realizing (belatedly and somewhat disgruntledly) that the time to grow up had finally arrived. The young, tan, beautiful couples who only a few years back arrived at parties with their dogs in the back seats of their sports cars now had children in tow and seemed to prowl around in Volvo station wagons.

Chestertown was changing too. Charlie Graves's Uptown Club would soon be an empty lot. Adkin's Lumber Company would be gone, another empty lot. The Five and Dime, too long irrelevant, would burn to the ground. The Chester Theater, whose balcony had long been cannibalized to replace the rotting seats below, would be perpetually dark. A lot of places that had gone to seed in the preceding years were steadily coming down. But what was going up?

Downtown, new brick sidewalks started to appear and the traffic lights, pulled down from their cables, began sprouting out of the sidewalks on wrought-iron poles. Queen and Water streets became forbidden territory to through traffic. (Even the old Queen Street entrance to town was closed.) Well-heeled out-of-towners were buying up property and sprucing the place up. At the edge of town, Wilmer Park was created from an old, swampy lot where twenty years earlier Lewis Kreworuka's dad let us race around in a beat-up Renault.

(The car, a four-seater, had an interior capacity fit for a driver, two midgets and a cat. Lewis, my brother Chris, Chuck Hayman, yours truly and at least two other pre-licensed teens would cram ourselves into the car and whip around the lot at blinding speeds, sometimes actually getting into second gear. There was a hairpin turn at the river's edge and whoever was driving was encouraged to hit that turn fast enough to bring the car up on two wheels. The rest of us would scream bloody murder and lean into the turn in the ridiculous notion that this alone would keep us from careening into the river.)

A new shopping center (sort of) materialized around a defunct discount store (Ames). A movie theater with postage stamp screens would get the public ready to invest in their own wide-screens TVs. (Now there's one for the conspiracy theorists!) Chinese food! (Need I say more?) A video store, so we could eat our Chinese food in front of our big-screen TVs while watching the latest teen slasher pic. No wonder the Eighties has such a reputation.

This decade, which gave us change and madness—good and bad—throughout the world, was a transforming decade for Chestertown as well. But like all transformations, sometimes it's true that you have to be careful what you wish for. You might get…

THE NINETIES

By 1991, we had bought a little house in College Heights and begun life as we now know it. Diane and I had two little kids, a dog, decent jobs, and I'm not ashamed to say it, breathed a huge sigh of relief that of all the places in the world, we were here.

Nineties for us seemed to bring a sense of normalcy that was just what the doctor ordered. But what of Chestertown? Was the town ready to settle into comfortable retirement, a coffee bar and La-Z-Boy on every corner? No way. Because the Nineties was to bring us a watershed moment (that lasted several years). A defining moment when the citizenry would be roused from its complacency to erect ramparts, gather the firebrands, call out the lawyers, write letters to the editor, take sides, rant about class warfare, show sincere (or feigned) interest in zoning regulations, call out more lawyers. Yes, it was…

The Battle Over Wal-Mart. Hard to believe that so much ire could be raised over a retailer known for inexpensive toilet paper, garden and panty hose, Chinese-made athletic shoes, laundry detergent, (well, the list goes on forever doesn't it, which is why so many people seem to love Wal-Mart).

Well, we know how it all turned out. Seems that the same company that has to spend millions on advertising just to let the world know that they are nice people (now there's a hint if I ever saw one) is the same company that couldn't give a hoot and a half (after the discount) about the wishes of the town they were about to invade and overwhelm.

Amazing wasn't it! Little ol' Chestertown stood up to a corporate entity the size of Microsoft and the Defense Department combined and said, "Thanks, but no thanks." I, for one, am glad they did. So what if I have to go to separate stores for toilet paper, extension cords, cough medicine and gift cards? The Battle Over Wal-Mart will forever remind me of why I like living here. Not all change is for the better.

There is nothing wrong with knowing the people at the grocery store, customers and clerks alike, well enough to say hello or even spend a minute or two talking about this or that. There is nothing wrong with looking forward to spending time and a few dollars at the Farmers' Market on Saturday, or sitting in the park sipping on a Stam's chocolate milkshake, or walking the dog through the college when the students are on vacation and the place is deserted and you can think about how many things are new and how many are exactly like you remember those distant years ago.

When I was in my teens, almost everyone I knew couldn't wait to get out of town, as if living here would lead to some sort of insidious mediocrity or worse. My own kids, now teenagers themselves, have a very different view. They like living here; they think Chestertown is a nice place to be. Me too.

Scrapbook

PAT HEROLD NIELSEN

It's there in all the photos –
The bright page on which we've written our happiest days.

Gleaming silver between distant trees,
kids tussling on the grass out front.

Lapis blue for Matt's first day alone in the skiff,
and the first turtle, and the first fish.

Blue-green for Judd, age three in his captain's hat,
steering the boat on his father's lap,

Boys dangling lines from a tilted dock,
soft faces washed in gold, waiting.

Here it is too:
the day my parents climbed in the pick-up,
and into the dinghy, and into the boat,
just to see a pink sunset.

In my favorite, faded now,
Ed stands on a high bank smiling,

his arms spread like William Blake's radiant man,
colors shooting out of his skin.

I saw that gesture once again years later,
on a brilliant sky blue day, again on the Chester.
The waterman who passed us saw us wave,
and waved back, and then in one perfect move
opened his arms wide and looked up to the heavens.
Then he glanced back at us and shook his head,
like a man who couldn't believe his good luck.

Of Crabs and Chicken-neckers, Bare Feet and Hurricanes, Out-of-Town Newspapers and Mister Foshnocks

ANDREW R. McCOWN

Editor's note: We sat down with Andrew R. McCown '77, Washington College alumnus, folklorist and storyteller, captain of the skipjack Elsworth, one-time waterman and now teacher of Bay sciences at Echo Hill Outdoor School. Our conversation is recounted here.

Has Chestertown changed much since you were a kid?

I was born in Chestertown in 1953 and there are a lot of things that are quite a bit different today than when I was growing up in the fifties and early sixties. We lived across the bridge, on the Queen Anne's side in the area called Kingstown, and it was a world apart.

In summertime the bridge was lined with people crabbing and fishing, whole families, thirty people or more on the sidewalk, set up with their crab traps and fishing rods for the day. It was commonplace to catch bushels of crabs and spend the whole day there. There'd be thirty to forty rowboats crabbing in the river. People would rent boats from the little marina that's still there just next to the Chester River Bridge.

And then around the corner to the north there was a place that we called Foshnocks. I really don't know the name of the people who ran it. I mean that was just what it sounded like to me when I was a kid, Foshnocks. And there were all of these people who came and rented boats for the weekends, and during the week too, primarily from Pennsylvania and New Jersey. They would hand-line for crabs. They would use just a cotton string and a chicken neck or a back of a chicken and a little weight. They would be in five to eight feet of water, anchor and put six or eight lines over the side. Then they would slowly pull the crab line up and if there was a crab on it they'd get it with a dip net. And they could catch bushels of crabs this way sitting there all day long.

You'd be a fool to attempt it today, because there are basically no crabs at Chestertown. I mean, every now and then we do get a small run of crabs that come up the river, but it'll be short-lived. You might see a waterman, might be up there three days, and then they've caught them, to the point it's not worth being there anymore.

The Chester River crab was thought to be sweeter than any of the other crabs, wasn't it?
Well, we considered the Chester River crab to be the biggest, fattest, sweetest crab that there was in the world. And we always heard stories, when we were kids, that the Wye River crab was the rival to the Chester River crab. But I choose not to engage in those arguments, because we knew what we knew, and there was just nothing like those heavy Chester River crabs. And you could buy bait at Larrimore Store, which was just after you came off the Chester River Bridge on the Queen Anne's shore. So for a lot of these people that would come down from Pennsylvania and New Jersey, this would probably be one of their first stops when they got here, to get frozen chicken necks. Larrimore Store was a great place with wooden floors and Coca Colas for a nickel, lots of penny candy, Squirrel Nuts and Mary Janes, and little pecan pies for a dime.

We would spend long days on the benches of Larrimore Store. Watching cars go by was one of our favorite pastimes. We would play a game to guess what kind of car was approaching. We didn't have the kind of traffic that exists now. In the distance we would see a car coming and guess what kind it was: a Ford, a Chevy, a Dodge or International Harvester, and really that's about all there was. There wasn't any such thing as foreign cars. All of the roads with the exception of 213, both north and south, were sandy dirt roads. I can remember when the county came in and first put some kind of pavement on those roads. We called it tar and chip. We all thought it was a terrible thing that they came and did that. It was hard on our feet, and it got so hot in the summertime it would get squishy, and you'd get tar on your bike.

I grew up there on the river, literally right on the river. I had four sisters. And there was quite a neighborhood of other kids at the time. The Anthonys, the Russells, the Joyces, the Carrolls, the Clarks, the Slagles. There were lots of summer games of kick the can. We had Anthony's pond, whenever it froze, for skating. Chestertown, when we were little, was a long walk across the bridge. The big thing for us was to go by boat. And since I lived right there on the river, my best friend Judge Anthony and I, as soon as we got old enough to start going across the river to Chestertown by boat, that's what we did. I bought my first boat when I was twelve. I took a loan from the bank, $300, and bought a motorboat that was just big enough for Judge and me to ski behind, and we skied incessantly. And gas was cheap. We could get a tank full of gas just by picking up bottles on the side of the road. Littering was just so much more commonplace, and we could get a nickel a bottle. I mean, you get five or six bottles and you got a gallon of gas.

One thing we didn't do was go barefoot in the river. It was too dangerous. It's quite amazing that's not the case today. I guess all that stuff has been water-worn and buried to the point that it's not there. That threat for the most part doesn't exist today. When I'm on the river with children today I insist that they wear sneakers, or something, but it's not because of glass, it's because of barnacles and tree limbs and things like that.

So we'd go to town by boat and tie up the boat to the foot of High Street. One of the big places for us to go was Fox's Five and Dime. You could get everything from yard goods and games to all kinds of housewares, but the big things for us were peashooters and cap guns. And I don't know if you could even buy a peashooter today. It's probably not legal anymore. But peashooters were such a big deal for us. We'd buy a bag of peas, you'd put them in your mouth and you'd shoot them through a straw.

My sisters and I would swim in the river. It was a soft sand bottom when we would go out to the end of the low tide and then two, three feet of mud. There were also rooted plants we called seaweed. And that would go out to about four feet deep. These plants were everywhere on both sides of the river, all the way from Crumpton to Chestertown. 'Course I didn't know it at the time, but it was a mix of wild celery, eelgrass and Eurasian milfoil that grew all the way to the surface. The milfoil was introduced to the bay I think in the late forties. The adults were always complaining about how bad the grass was, how thick it was, a menace to all the sailors and motor boaters because it would get caught in the props. I can't remember ever hearing anything positive about the rooted plants growing along the shoreline, about it being part of the ecology or the system. But that had a great deal to do with why there were so many crabs.

You know what wiped it out?
Well, after Hurricane Agnes, in 1972, we got tremendous sediment loads in the bay. But I think it would be wrong to blame it all on Agnes. If you read [Susan Q. Stranahan's] *Susquehanna, River of Dreams*, it talks about our changing land use through all of Pennsylvania setting the stage for disaster in terms of sediment erosion. It was just a matter of time before a massive storm like Agnes was going to dump that kind of water through the middle of Pennsylvania. And the sediments were devastating to the bay. It was hot, and we got very stagnant water for a long time, and then it was a steady decline after that. The bay used to have 600,000 acres of grass beds, and now we're at something like 50,000 or 60,000 acres. It's pretty grim. The last time I saw major grass beds in the Chester River even as far up as Quaker Neck Landing was in about 1975. Oh, there are little pockets of some grass beds, and people involved in surveys get all excited. But by comparison, the river, in my opinion, is completely void of grasses.

There aren't a lot of commercial fishermen on the Chester any-more. In this part of the river there are just three, Sammy Joiner, Dicky Manning—and he doesn't even fish anywhere up near this far—and Steve Cohey. These guys are what are called pound net fishermen.

When I was a kid, gill netting was legal in the river. A gill net is fixed so the head of the fish goes through the opening of the net but it can't go any further through and when it goes to back out with its gills open, it gets caught. So they would put stakes out and then attach gill nets to them. If you went across the Chester River Bridge in the spring and looked north, there would be hundreds of stakes. You had to wonder how a fish could get up the river.

And you would catch forty- and fifty-pound rockfish. It was quite extraordinary what the river would yield at that time. There were commercial crabbers besides all the tourists out there hand-crabbing. Nobody works that anymore, there's no point to it.

Chestertown was a waterman's town?
Yes it was. There were a lot of African-American watermen, and their houses were the little row houses. Some of them are the saltboxes that are on Water Street, where there's a lot of renaissance right now, behind the Chestertown Marina. It was a waterman's town to a very different degree. The river had a lot more activity than it does now. The river was a lot more important in a lot of ways. The Chestertown Marina had a railway. Dicky Manning tells me he used to hand-tong for oysters just next to the country club.

There were so many crabs, my friends and I would spend a half a day just going from piling to piling under the Chester River Bridge, catching crabs on the dip net. You could catch peelers all day long like that. You'd be a fool to even attempt to look nowadays 'cause they're never there. That's really one of the saddest things I know, the disappearance of crabs in the river, and now oysters, too, in the lower part of the river. Now there are no oysters that are commercially viable or maybe not even in existence upriver of Quaker Neck Landing. It's a really sad thing. I mean there were a lot of oysters out there and a lot of watermen. They're all gone.

If you look at Chestertown, it is just a picturesque colonial town, a beautiful riverfront town with magnificent colonial homes strung along the river. Some changes are really positive. The town looks better than it did when I was a kid. All the sidewalks are brick. There's been a lot of renovation and restoration of older buildings, and it looks terrific. But the river, it looks good, but it's worse. It seems like such a robbery. And it seems wrong to settle for less. With a really productive healthy river, this could be so much more than just a beautiful town with a lot of memories of what things really used to be like.

Whatever became of Foshnock's and his chicken-neckers?
I'm not sure I should finish that story, how it will look in print. But my memory is there were two places on the Queen Anne's shore where weekend crabbers would come down from Pennsylvania and New Jersey, and they would rent rowboats to go out crabbing. Sometimes we felt they were so rude because on a high tide they literally might be ten feet off our windows—whole boatloads of overweight people from New Jersey with AM radios on and crab lines all over the place.

You know, looking back on it, they had all the right in the world to be there. It was public water. We didn't think of it that way. There might be thirty or forty of these boats that would be in the river out in front of my parents' house, and they'd all be crowded. And one of these marinas was just two properties upriver from us and to the best of my recollection, it was owned by a guy by the name of Foshnock. I really don't know how it was spelled. I didn't spell in those days—that's just what it sounded like to me. It wasn't a full-blown marina, mostly just a place for these rowboats and weekend crabbers from Pennsylvania and New Jersey, and it was well known to us that's where all of these people came from.

The property just on the other side of Foshnock's was owned by Bob Fleetwood, an insurance salesman in Chestertown. Bob Fleetwood was a big guy, like 6'3", always exciting to be around. Apparently he didn't like Mr. Foshnock and his crowd of crabbers so much. They would make a lot of noise early in the morning, and he let it be known that he didn't like putting up with their trash or their noise.

One Sunday morning he walked out to the end of his pier, and there was a section of a Sunday paper, and neatly placed in the center of it was a pile of human waste. Bob Fleetwood was infuriated, and he stormed over to Mr. Foshnock's and demanded that he come and see what Mr. Foshnock's people had left him. And he walked him out there and pointed at this offering that had been left there, and he said, "You see what your people have done? You see what your people have left here on my pier?"

And Mr. Foshnock looked down at it, and looked back up at Bob Fleetwood and said, "That's not my people."

Bob Fleetwood said, "How do you know that?"

"Well just look," said Mr. Foshnock, "that's on the *Washington Post*. My people are all from Pennsylvania and New Jersey. They never get the *Washington Post*."

And you know the funny thing about this, you couldn't buy the *Washington Post* or the *Philadelphia Inquirer* in Chestertown in those days. So whoever did it came from far away. And it was commonly known that people from Washington, they seemed to frequent other parts of the county, all the way out to Rock Hall. They'd drive through here, but this was definitely a New Jersey, Pennsylvania spot. So it was a very funny argument. Mr. Fleetwood got a huge kick out of it, and he spread the story all over Chestertown.

Here, on the Chester

MEREDITH DAVIES HADAWAY

Wind sweeps the river's
secrets down to shell and mud

and air. Three herons stroll through puddles
after minnow-spark. Straddling rock

and sand, a sycamore drops its mottled bark
on a bank that soon

will disappear. Rivers grow larger, rivers grow
small. Here, where the dead like pebbles rise

among the weeds, I'll build my house
on water.

Tea and Infamy: Fact, Fiction and the Mysterious Spring of 1774

ADAM GOODHEART

MAY 23, 1774, is a legendary date in Chestertown's history.

If you had been standing at the foot of High Street on that day, you might have seen the local Sons of Liberty stealthily assemble, one by one, at the dockside to strike a blow against tyranny. Beyond them, anchored just off the town wharf, you might have seen the looming masts of the brigantine *Geddes*, newly arrived in port with a cargo of the hated tea that King George's ministers had taxed—tea that the patriots of the Thirteen Colonies had vowed would never sully their breakfast tables. You might have heard the faint creak of muffled oars, and then the startled cries of sailors surprised at their posts. You might have seen a desperate shipboard melee—and then heard several splashes as the crates of tea, followed by the sailors themselves, were tossed into the muddy water of the Chester River.

On the other hand, you might not have.

The problem is that no one today can find a scrap of contemporary evidence to prove that the Chestertown Tea Party ever happened. The story has been told—and greatly embellished—by generations of townsfolk. It has been enshrined in local histories, and thence picked up nationwide in tourist guides, textbooks and even scholarly works.

Even the Library of Congress's website mentions it as an episode on our nation's road to independence. And of course, every spring thousands of tourists flock to Chestertown to witness a reenactment of the Tea Party, accompanied by parades, pageantry and raft races. But there is no known 18th-century letter, diary, court record or newspaper account describing or even mentioning what is supposed to have occurred here.

I had heard the story of the Tea Party since my first day in Chestertown, nearly three years ago. I'd repeated it unhesitatingly to friends, students and out-of-town visitors, especially since my Washington College office is in the Custom House, a few yards away from where it is supposed to have occurred. I never thought to question the conventional wisdom until the spring of 2005, when I taught a course called "Chestertown's America," which surveyed four centuries of our country's history from the vantage point of this small Eastern Shore town. In teaching the class, I relied largely on primary sources (since almost no serious scholarship exists on the history of Kent County), and so when I prepared for the section on the American Revolution, I set out to look for documents about the Chestertown Tea Party.

But when I played the old historian's game of follow-the-footnotes—working my way back along a trail of references to find the original sources of the story—my pursuit hit a dead end in the late 19th century. Inquiries among local experts and archivists drew a blank. A search among the surviving records of early Chestertown (assisted by an enterprising student, Erin Koster, who wrote her term paper on the Tea Party legend) also failed to find any conclusive proof. Friends started warning me, only half-jokingly, that I'd better watch my back around town: people around here can take the colonial past pretty seriously. A few reminded me about the *Simpsons* episode where Lisa discovers the secret pirate confessions of her town's revered founder, Jebediah Springfield, and ends up as a target for historical-society hit men.

By this time, however, I was hooked on the mystery, hit men or no. And our search was starting to turn up some pretty tantalizing hints and clues—circumstantial evidence of what may or may not have happened here in May of 1774. In the process, I found myself delving deep into the 18th century, and into the life of a small town in the not-yet-united colonies of British North America, during the final spring before the world turned upside down.

* * *

WHAT IS BEYOND DISPUTE is that Chestertown that spring was abuzz with revolutionary—and anti-revolutionary—excitement. For nearly a decade, some of the town's leading citizens had been involved in protesting the "taxation without representation" imposed by the mother country on her American colonies. They had worked successfully to help overturn the Stamp Act of 1765, which had placed a duty on all newspapers, government documents and printed matter—only to see it replaced a few years later by even more onerous import fees on glass, lead, paint, paper and tea. And recently, the flames of local indignation had been fanned afresh.

The gentry of Chestertown—stolid Water Street burghers like Thomas Smyth III of Widehall and Thomas Ringgold V of the Hynson-Ringgold House—might have seemed unlikely revolutionaries. They came from families of socially reactionary, culturally Anglophile tobacco planters, deeply rooted for more than a century in the soil of Kent County—families so hidebound that Thomas followed Thomas, generation after generation, as if each eldest son were a clone of the father who had preceded him, in an undifferentiated cycle of assemblymen, vestrymen, justices of the peace.

Moreover, there was an even more salient fact that might undercut these men's credentials as freedom fighters: they were almost all of them slaveowners. By the time of the Revolution, nearly half the people in Kent County were black, and were legally classified not as persons but as property; as late as 1770, maritime records reveal, slave ships still occasionally landed at the town wharf at the foot of High Street. Indeed, Ringgold's father had made much of his fortune running slavers from West Africa to the Chesapeake—a business that he oversaw with grim efficiency from his hulking mansion near the wharf, the building now known (erroneously) as the Custom House. The elder Thomas Ringgold's papers are infused with a sense of what would, in a later century, be termed "the banality of evil." In a 1761 letter, he noted with cold calculation that aboard one of his ships, which had left the Slave Coast with 320 men, women and children, conditions in the Middle Passage had been so bad that by the time the vessel arrived in the Chesapeake, "we had but 105 left alive to sell, 11 of them so bad we were glad to get 11 pounds per Head for them." And yet, just a few years after penning these words, he would defend American liberty as a Maryland delegate to the Stamp Act Congress in Philadelphia. Thomas Ringgold IV died in 1772, passing this ambivalent legacy—along with his large fortune and the two houses on Water Street—to his son, Thomas V.

Kent County could be a harsh and authoritarian place for whites as well as blacks. Justice was summarily dispensed at twice-annual sittings of the county court, by jurymen who were selected from among a small pool of well-to-do landowners. Sentences (almost always inflicted on those of a lower social class) included floggings, the pillory, brandings and sometimes public hangings at the town gallows. Not just at the time of the Revolution but, for many decades afterward, Chestertown's social order often seemed more medieval than democratic. (Indeed, the property ownership requirement for voting in town elections was not revoked until the 1960s.)

Yet for all the staunch conservatism of Chestertown and its Eastern Shore surroundings, the decades leading up to 1774 had brought momentous changes. Around mid-century, the tobacco farming of the colony's earliest years gave way to a new, more reliable and lucrative crop: wheat. Before long, the grain and flour of the Upper Shore reached markets in the Caribbean and across the Atlantic, bringing a new degree of prosperity to Kent and neighboring counties—and with this prosperity, a new sophistication, even cosmopolitanism. Handsome new brick houses appeared along the sloping, muddy streets of Chestertown. Vessels from Lisbon, Genoa, Barbados and other exotic ports of call anchored at the wharf. The town hosted performances by Shakespearean actors and a scientific demonstration of the newly-discovered marvel of electricity. Local gentry began to hold balls, race thoroughbred horses, take social excursions to Philadelphia and Annapolis, and even to read books and periodicals from London and beyond.

And so, on the eve of the Revolution, the Chestertown scene included not just the familiar Smyths and Ringgolds, but also the likes of William Carmichael, a rakish young bachelor from Round Top plantation, just across the river in Queen Anne's County. Carmichael's wealthy father, who possessed one of the largest private libraries in the colony, had sent him off to read classical literature at the University of Edinburgh, where the young man had imbibed both the principles of the Scottish Enlightenment and a sense of romantic identification with the republican heroes of ancient Greece and Rome. (On his finger, Carmichael wore a signet ring with an emblem of his own invention: a hand brandishing a spear beneath the motto "MANUS HAEC INIMICA TYRANNIS"—"This hand is the enemy of tyrants.")

Another sign of the new worldliness was the just-completed mansion that Thomas Smyth had built overlooking the town wharf. Widehall (as it would be dubbed in the 20th century) was a house on a scale unlike anything Chestertown had seen, but even more important, its architecture spoke to new role models and aspirations. The front door echoed the architecture of a Greek temple, the high-ceilinged parlors were adorned with cornices and architraves in the Roman style, and the main hall flaunted a columned arcade that might have come straight from the courtyard of a Florentine palazzo. There was nothing cramped or colonial about this house—nor, we may well suppose, about the mentality of its proprietor, the largest landowner and shipowner in the county.

Chestertown's residents had always considered themselves loyal Englishmen—supporting British efforts in the French and Indian War, faithfully toasting the King's health over bowls of punch, and marking royal birthdays during services in the Anglican church on the market square. But that loyalty had come under increasing strain. In 1758, when seven companies of redcoats took up winter quarters in Chestertown, their presence caused such tension that a pitched brawl broke out among soldiers, sailors and local youths—ending in the death of a sailor and murder charges against two sons of prominent families. Moreover, many Kent Countians already had such deep roots in the New World that it had been three or four generations since anyone had set foot in the mother country. The ancestral tie to England grew slightly weaker with each passing year.

So by the early 1770s, as the whole English-speaking world followed the tumultuous events in Boston—a city already in near-rebellion against the Crown—it is not so surprising that many Marylanders identified more with their fellow colonists 400 miles to the north than with political leaders across the ocean. The Eastern Shore, as yet, had no newspaper of its own, but its inhabitants read the Annapolis and Philadelphia papers, which reported exhaustively on the news from New England: the growing civil unrest, the military occupation of Boston, the deadly melee between redcoats and street ruffians (reminiscent of what had happened in Chestertown a dozen years before) and finally the dumping of East India Company tea into Boston Harbor.

As representatives from all thirteen colonies began assembling to confront the crisis, many of them passed through Kent County, which happened to lie on one of the eastern seaboard's main overland routes. Travelers from the rest of Maryland, from Virginia, and from other points south would be ferried across the Bay from Annapolis to Rock Hall, where they would continue on horseback through Chestertown (often stopping there for food, drink and lodging) and then up the peninsula to Philadelphia and points north; they would come back again on their return. Thus the town became not just a rest stop on the colonial I-95, as it were, but also a segment of the information highway by which news passed among the previously disconnected provinces.

In September 1774, for instance, we find Carmichael writing to a friend about a supper he had attended the night before at "Tom Ringgold's" house: "Young Carroll of Carrollton was there in high spirits from Philadelphia. [He reports] General Gage intrenching himself in Boston afraid to leave the city & sea, I wish it may prove so. Lee is now at Philadelphia, crying Havoc & Let slip the dogs of War ..." Charles Carroll of Carrollton and Richard Henry Lee, then both members of the first Continental Congress (and both later to become signers of the Declaration of Independence), were rising revolutionary stars whose names and faces obviously were already familiar to Chestertown.

Indeed, in that same dining room the previous year, Ringgold had entertained another distinguished traveler from across the Bay: Colonel George Washington, passing through on his way to deliver his stepson to college in New York. Unfortunately, no record of the conversation at that 1773 gathering survives, but one can easily imagine the Virginian holding forth to Ringgold and his guests about the alarming state of current politics.

* * *

RINGGOLD, CARMICHAEL AND SMYTH were almost certainly among the "number of respectable gentlemen—friends to liberty" who gathered at a local tavern (probably Worrell's, at the corner of Queen and Cannon streets) on May 13, 1774. The men had come together in an emergency meeting to respond to late-breaking developments in Boston, in London—and in Chestertown itself.

The only account of that day's events is maddeningly vague—a report that an unknown participant sent the following week to Annapolis for publication in the *Maryland Gazette*. His grandiloquent dispatch began with a poetic quotation from Joseph Addison's play *Cato*, about the Roman statesman who defended the republic (unsuccessfully) against the upstart tyrant Caesar:

> Remember, O my friends, the laws, the rights,
> The gen'rous plan of pow'r deliver'd down
> From age to age, by your renown'd forefathers;
> So dearly bought, the price of so much blood!
> O! Let it never perish in your hands,
> But piously transmit it to your children.

In this same spirit—of what might be called revolutionary conservatism—the Chestertown "friends to liberty" continued by asserting their staunch loyalty to the ancient constitution of Great Britain ("the most perfect under heaven"). But they also condemned the "corrupt and despotic ministry" that currently held sway in London, and called for a mass meeting of Kent County's citizens on May 18 to formulate a local response to the tea tax.

It was at that second meeting, held at the Kent County courthouse, that the participants read and approved the six declarations that came to be known as the Chestertown Resolves. First—for this was not yet an all-out rebellion—they acknowledged their allegiance to George III. Second, they swore enmity to all taxation without representation. Third, they asserted that Parliament's tea tax had been "calculated to *enslave* the Americans." Fourth, they agreed that any citizens found importing or purchasing dutiable tea "shall be stigmatized as enemies to the liberties of America." Fifth, they pledged to enforce these resolutions among their neighbors—if necessary, by shunning them for refusal to comply. Finally, they decided to disseminate these Resolves to the press.

And at the bottom of that column in the *Gazette*, the following brief and cryptic postscript appeared:

> N.B. The above resolves were entered into upon a discovery of a late importation of dutiable tea, (in the brigantine Geddes, of this port) for some of the neighbouring counties. Further measures are in contemplation, in consequence of a late and *very* alarming act of parliament.

Those two sentences are the only contemporary record that even hints at the Chestertown Tea Party as it is traditionally recounted today. The next news from Kent County in the *Maryland Gazette* came two weeks later, in a report on yet another mass meeting at the courthouse held on June 2. This time, the citizens appointed a local "Committee of Correspondence" (with Smyth as chairman, and Carmichael and Ringgold among its members) to share information with patriots in the other colonies and to work toward the repeal of the hated Parliamentary acts—a measure being taken in dozens of communities throughout America.[1] There was no mention whatsoever of anything resembling a tea party, or indeed of the fate of the offending tea found on the *Geddes*—and the *Gazette*, the province's only newspaper, carried almost no news from Chestertown during the rest of the spring and summer.

Other possible sources are equally unhelpful or, worse, nonexistent. There are no known diaries from Chestertown during the period. The surviving minutes of the county court do not begin until November 1774. A few private letters written from Chestertown in May and June have turned up—including by Thomas Ringgold and Thomas Smyth—but these are mostly business correspondence, and mention nothing about the tea controversy.

Perhaps one day an intrepid researcher will find the proverbial smoking gun, in the form of a letter or diary that now sits forgotten in a corner of someone's attic, or even in an archive or library. Until then, however, the only thing to do is assemble the clues and play detective: in particular, to scrutinize that cryptic two-line postscript in the *Gazette* as closely as possible, examine the context in which it appeared, look for corroborating evidence, and try to decode its true meaning.

"the brigantine Geddes ..."

The *Geddes* turns up in the 18th-century records of His Majesty's customs officers as a locally-built ship of fifty tons burden, one of the smaller vessels plying the trans-Atlantic routes. ("Brigantine" is a term for a two-masted vessel with square sails on the foremast, but not aft.) A search through the neatly-ruled columns of entries at the "port of Chester" for the spring of 1774—records that were believed until recently not to have survived—reveals that on May 7, the brig arrived at her home anchorage after a crossing from London; her captain, John Harrison, commanded a crew of seven men. The cargo's owner is listed as "Jas. Nicholson." As to its contents, the customs officer originally wrote "European Goods per cockets." (Cockets were

---

[1] The following were the members of Kent County's Committee of Correspondence, appointed at the June 2 meeting: Thomas Smyth (chairman), William Ringgold (of Eastern Neck), Robert Buchanan, John Maxwell, Emory Sudler, Col. Richard Lloyd, Col. Joseph Nicholson, John Cadwalader, Joseph Nicholson, Jr., Thomas Ringgold, Thomas Bedingfield Hands, Joseph Earle, Ezekiel Foreman, James Anderson, James Hynson, James Pearce, Isaac Spencer, William Carmichael, John Vorhees, Donaldson Yeates, William Ringgold (of Chestertown), Eleazer McComb, Dr. John Scott, Jeremiah Nicols, Dr. William Bordley, Capt. James Nicholson.

separate manifests that would have listed the cargo in greater detail.) Then, after penning these words, he went back, inserted a carat after the word "European," and wrote above it the tiny letters "& E.I." This abbreviation stood for "East India": in other words, possibly spices, possibly silk, possibly china—and possibly tea. The *Geddes* departed Chestertown again on May 24, this time bound for Madeira with a cargo of wheat and flour.

"of this port ..."

The customs records do not reveal the name of the *Geddes's* owner, and her possible connection to William Geddes, a local merchant who also served as Chestertown's customs collector, cannot be proven. More interesting is the identification of James Nicholson as the owner of the brig's cargo—including, most likely, the tea. The thirty-seven-year-old Nicholson was a prominent native of Chestertown who had grown up in the house that is now the White Swan Tavern. (In fact, he seems to have been one of the two youths who was accused of killing the sailor in 1758, and then pardoned.) A veteran of the Royal Navy in the French and Indian War, he had returned to his hometown as a shipping merchant several years earlier. And he was, at least on the surface, no Tory—in fact, he affixed his name to the Chestertown Resolves and was appointed to the Committee of Correspondence. Nicholson's involvement adds an extra twist to an already-perplexing tale.

"a late and very alarming act of parliament..."

This was almost certainly the Boston Port Bill, which Parliament had passed in late March; word of it reached America just around the time that the Chestertown Resolves were being drafted. (In fact, the *Geddes* herself, ironically enough, may well have brought the news to Chestertown.) This law's passage had—to use a word that was coming into vogue at the time—electrified the colonists. The Port Bill ordered that until such time as the people of Boston paid the tea tax and reimbursed the East India Company for its spoiled goods, the city's harbor would be closed to all commercial shipping. Not a box or bale would be unloaded at Long Wharf; not a single brig or schooner would set sail past Castle William into Massachusetts Bay. It is understandable that this news had a particularly shocking effect among the shipping merchants of Chestertown, some of whom traded with New England.

"Further measures are in contemplation ..."

Most tantalizing of all is the question of what was meant by these ominous-sounding "further measures ... in contemplation" on account of the Port Bill news. It has been suggested, naturally, that this must refer to the Tea Party. But it seems more straightforward to conclude that it simply referred to the appointment of the Committee of Correspondence, as reported in the *Gazette* two weeks later. Dumping tea into the Chester River would have been a logical response to the Tea Act, not the Port Bill—and it seems highly unlikely that the would-be perpetrators, had they been contemplating such a deed, would have advertised it ahead of time in the newspaper.

Along similar lines, if the Tea Party did occur, why was it not reported afterwards in the press? It might be argued that the *Gazette*—a four-page weekly newspaper—was often spotty in its coverage, especially of Eastern Shore news. Or perhaps the "respectable gentlemen" of the Committee of Correspondence were embarrassed by the outburst of mob violence in their town. But the Tea Party in Boston Harbor had, in the six months since its occurrence, been imitated in towns up and down the Atlantic seaboard, and had invariably made headlines; the May 5 issue of the *Gazette* carried a laudatory account of one such recent incident in New York. Newspapers as far away as Rhode Island ran reports of the Chestertown Resolves. So if the Chestertown Tea Party was indeed a copycat crime—and if the local patriots were, as it seems from their Resolves, so eager to intimidate suspected Tories—why not trumpet it as widely as possible?

And yet ... multiple sources make it clear that the *Geddes* was in the right place at the right time. It also seems almost certain that she was indeed carrying tea, and that this tea was discovered by local patriot leaders. Once they had found the illicit crates, how likely is it that they would have allowed it to land, given the political atmosphere in Chestertown at the time? Similarly, would they have allowed Captain Harrison to sail away with the tea, only to unload it at some other port? What, indeed, could they have done *but* toss it into the Chester River?

So imagine a slightly different scenario from the one that is reenacted at the foot of High Street every Memorial Day weekend. Imagine, let us say, that Captain Harrison had loaded the tea in London of his own accord, with Nicholson unaware of its presence until it reached Maryland on May 7. Imagine it being discovered—perhaps by a pilot or longshoreman in Chestertown, perhaps even by Nicholson himself—as the brig's cargo was unloaded. Imagine the town abuzz with the news, and its leading merchants hastily convening at Worrell's Tavern on May 13, anxious to confront the crisis and dismayed at being branded as secret Tories. Imagine them—emboldened, perhaps, by the consumption of some non-dutiable beverages—heading from the tavern straight down to where the *Geddes* lay at anchor, boarding her, and, with Nicholson's consent (or even active participation), hurling the crates of tea into the river. Then imagine that they kept the details of the story out of the press in order not to embarrass one of their own, publishing just enough to confirm Chestertown's loyalty to the patriot cause.

It could all quite possibly have happened this way. But did it?

* * *

THE EARLIEST DEFINITE MENTION of the Chestertown Tea Party that I discovered was in a slim paperbound volume, *Gem City on the Chester,* published locally in 1898. Its author, Frederick G. Usilton, was a newspaper editor and enthusiastic booster of his hometown—and the kind of journalist who never let the truth stand in the way of a good story. His account of the Tea Party ran as follows:

> The brigantine *Geddes* arrived at Chestertown in 1774 with a small cargo of dutiable tea for some of the neighboring counties. The inhabitants assembled in town meeting on May 13, and

held indignation meetings and threw the tea overboard. This same day the tea was thrown overboard in Boston Harbor.

Given his phrasing, Usilton clearly had read the coverage in the *Gazette*. But he is far from being a very trustworthy narrator, starting with the fact that—as any schoolchild then, if not now, could have told him—the Boston Tea Party happened in December 1773, six months before the allegedly simultaneous event in Chestertown. His other writings are similarly riddled with errors and exaggerations. And yet all of the current references to the Chestertown Tea Party—in books, articles and even respectable academic publications—can ultimately be traced to that passage of Usilton's, later reprinted in his more widely circulated 1916 *History of Kent County, Maryland*, and thence picked up in a 1932 article in the prestigious *Maryland Historical Magazine*, which lent it (undeservedly) a certain scholarly luster.

The year 1898 was still close enough to the Revolution that elderly inhabitants of Kent County might well have heard firsthand accounts of the Tea Party from their grandparents or great-grandparents. On the other hand, as with many family stories—especially when little is written down—the details may have gotten muddled through the years. Perhaps memories of the excitement in town over tea—the Resolves and the patriotic meetings—had slowly morphed into something more dramatic, more closely resembling the famous events at Boston. Perhaps the locals had unwittingly borrowed their story from nearby Annapolis, where in the fall of 1774, patriots burned the ship *Peggy Stewart* to the waterline after finding a cargo of tea onboard. (This event was well-documented in contemporary newspaper articles, letters and memoirs.)

Or Usilton may simply have made it all up. At the end of the 19th century, when he wrote his book, America was in the midst of one of its periodic fits of colonial nostalgia: groups like the Daughters of the American Revolution were being founded, historic reenactments were being staged, and 18th-century American antiques were collected for the very first time. Towns and villages throughout the East avidly sought their own distinctive claims to Revolutionary fame—and in the absence of anything factual, many weren't above shameless invention. *Gem City on the Chester* clearly aimed to attract tourists and boost local pride, and a quaint tea party story suited its goals quite nicely. Its author may have come across the ambiguous 1774 *Gazette* article and decided to craft it into a more marketable commodity.

Decades later, during another national bout of Revolutionary fever—as the country approached its Bicentennial—the Tea Party again took center stage. In 1967, a group of Kent Countians organized the first-ever Tea Party Festival, which drew colonial buffs, craft vendors and 25,000 tourists, and has been repeated every year since.[2] Most visitors have come away with little more sense of history than a glimpse of tea crates and tricorn hats floating in the river, while for most locals, it's been simply an opportunity to do some hearty drinking and carousing (which, today as in the 18th century, few locals are wont to pass up), as well as perhaps to make a bit of money. The true past slumbers through these festivities undisturbed.

* * *

YET THE CHESTERTOWN TEA PARTY is still one of those stories that—whether true or false in the most literal sense—have their own innate authenticity. To walk the streets of Chestertown today is to be transported into another century, and to catch glimpses of the world into which our nation was born—a world in which native ground and personal identity were synonymous, in which political debates were hammered out over cups of coffee or mugs of beer, and in which history's great changes arrived slowly, almost stealthily, drifting up the river with the tide.

No Revolutionary battles were fought here, besides some minor guerrilla skirmishes between local militiamen and bands of marauding

---

[2] It is unclear when and why the traditional date of the Tea Party was switched from May 13 to May 23. This may simply have been someone's slip of the pen, or a historian's attempt to have it accord better with the "further measures ... under contemplation" on May 19, or, most cynically of all, simply a 20th-century effort to push it closer to Memorial Day weekend.

Tories. Kent County's most important contribution to the war effort was probably its supplying of grain to the Continental Army—hardly the sort of thing to inspire tourist festivals and reenactments. The closest thing to a glimpse of major drama came on Sunday, August 25, 1777, when, if you had been standing near the mouth of Worton Creek, you would have seen a breathtaking sight: an armada of some 260 British warships anchored just offshore, on their way up the Bay bringing troops to attack Philadelphia.

In Chestertown and its environs, the American Revolution often felt less like a clash of nations than—in keeping with the spirit of the Tea Party story—like a conflict among neighbors, one that divided families and communities in much the same way that the Civil War would do here almost a century later. "I fear our peaceful Days in America throughout are over," wrote Thomas Ringgold in the fall of 1774, and he was right. By the following year, residents of Chestertown had to choose once and for all which side they were on—and be prepared to suffer the consequences. When a local minister publicly complained about the revolutionary government of Maryland, remarking "that there was more liberty in Turkey than in this province," he was arrested and hauled off to Annapolis under armed guard. Another Kent County loyalist, James Chalmers, raised and commanded an entire regiment of Delmarva Tories, who fought against Washington at the battle of Monmouth—only to end up after the war as miserable exiles or prisoners, with their property confiscated and their former British protectors vanquished.

The wartime role of the brig *Geddes*, if any, is lost to history: after the putative Tea Party, she appears once more in Chestertown before the records of His Majesty's Customs in Maryland abruptly stop in the spring of 1775, never to resume. But as for those Kent Countians whom the vessel and her cargo had moved to an act of patriotism—that is, the signers of the Chestertown Resolves—a number went on to more glorious deeds. Ringgold helped to draw up the constitution for the new state of Maryland before his untimely death in 1776. Thomas Smyth also served in the constitutional convention, built warships at his Chester River boatyard, and lost most of his fortune—including

Widehall—by devoting it to the Revolution. William Carmichael, who left Chestertown for Europe shortly before war broke out, spent most of his colorful career there, where he recruited Lafayette to the American cause, assisted Franklin and Jay in their diplomatic endeavors, served as minister to Spain, and became one of America's first overseas secret agents. John Cadwalader rose to a generalship in the Continental Army, and fought a famous duel in defense of George Washington.

But perhaps the most intriguing epilogue of all is that involving James Nicholson, the Chestertown native, pardoned murderer, Royal Navy veteran—and owner of the tea aboard the *Geddes*. On June 6, 1776, when the Continental Congress announced the first captains appointed to the brand-new United States Navy, the name at the head of the list was none other than Nicholson's. (Clearly, any suspicions of Toryism that might have lingered in Chestertown had not reached Philadelphia.) As the most senior captain and commodore-in-chief in the Navy, Nicholson seemed poised to attain a brilliant military career and undying fame. Instead, he ended up with a singularly inglorious one, and a well-merited obscurity. Entrusted with command of the 28-gun frigate *Virginia*, he endlessly procrastinated on actually taking her to sea, finding one excuse after another to remain safe in harbor. When after almost two years of this he finally bestirred himself to sail, he had barely cleared the mouth of the Chesapeake before he ran the *Virginia* aground on a shoal, where she and her entire crew were promptly captured by a British warship without firing a single shot.

Was Captain Nicholson playing a double game all along? Could his former neighbors in Kent County have told the distinguished gentlemen of the Continental Congress a few things that would have made their wigs curl? Perhaps it is fanciful even to wonder. But after more than two centuries, this may be the final mystery surrounding the Chestertown Tea Party—a question whose answer lies with the bones of the brig *Geddes*, on some Eastern Shore riverbed or distant reef.

Allen Ginsberg Levitates Chestertown

ROBERT DAY

SINCE THE EARLY 1970s, Chestertown has been host to hundreds of literary figures from all over the world, including scores of Pulitzer Prize and National Book Award winners, half a dozen or so Poet Laureates, plus four winners of the Nobel Prize in Literature: Toni Morrison, Joseph Brodsky, Derek Walcott and J.M. Coetzee.

Among the other literary greats brought in by Washington College were the playwrights Edward Albee and Israel Horowitz; the French author Alain Robbe-Grillet; the poets William Stafford, Carolyn Forché, Henry Taylor, James Dickey, James Tate, Billy Collins, Dave Smith and Lawrence Ferlinghetti; the Woody Allen screenplay writer Walter Bernstein; novelists Anthony Burgess, George Garrett, J.R. Salamanca; fiction writers such as William Gass, Mavis Gallant (of *New Yorker* fame), Joyce Carol Oates; plus our own William Warner, Chris Tilghman, Douglass Wallop and John Barth. And that isn't the half of it. Just typing the list I realize I left off the poets Richard Wilbur, Donald Justice, Marvin Bell, Anthony Hecht and Gwendolyn Brooks—as well as perhaps the finest American short story writer of the 20th century: Katherine Anne Porter.

Not all of these writers ventured into Chestertown for any length of time, but many of them did. I remember walking to the White Swan Tavern one day to pick up Joseph Brodsky (he had come to Washington College with his translators, Anthony Hecht and Derek Walcott) and before I got there I found Derek Walcott browsing through the Compleat Bookseller. As I was early, I stopped in and Walcott talked a bit about the books he was buying (a copy of John Barth's *Letters* if I remember correctly, plus William Warner's *Beautiful Swimmers*).

Going out of the store, he asked me to walk him around town, and I did; he wanted to hear "apocryphal" stories of Chestertown and so I told him the one about how the local paper once carried the headline: "Baltimore Woman Dies at 92," referring to a woman who had come here when she was two and lived the rest of her life in town but alas, was never considered a native, by the natives. I told other tales as well, some of them irreverent and politically incorrect, and he seemed to like those best.

When we got back to the White Swan, Brodsky and Hecht were in a debate about some translation problem in one of Brodsky's poems and asked Walcott to settle it, which Walcott did by first looking at the Russian text of Brodsky's poem, then at Hecht's translation of the line, then at Brodsky's translation of the same line. After a moment Walcott fished a coin out of his pocket and flipped it: heads Anthony Hecht, tails Brodsky. Brodsky won. In such ways are Nobel Prize-winning poems translated by Nobel Prize-winning poets. On High Street in Chestertown no less.

Later all four of us walked around, and the three of them recited various lines of Brodksy's poetry, sometimes in Russian, and then in various translations. When we got to the town dock, Walcott retold a few of the stories I had previously told him, and Brodsky recited a poem to the river. As it was in Russian I had, of course, no notion why the Chester River should inspire the recitation of a poem, but it did: I do remember a waterman in his bateau looked at us, no doubt sure we were from "up to the College."

There were other writers who took time off from their duties at the College to walk into Chestertown. In the early seventies, William

Stafford (the only poet to get an honorary degree from Washington College) wanted to see the Chester River, and at the town dock he also recited a few lines of poetry, this one (in English) being:

"What the river says, that is what I say," which is the final line of his famous poem "Ask Me."

A few years later Katherine Anne Porter and I were walking from the College to the home of Norman and Alice James for dinner when she wanted to know if we could get a bottle of Virginia Gentleman at the Past Time Bar (now Andy's); we could not, as it turned out, so she got it the next day on our way out of town. She did, however, stand me for "three fingers" of the "bar's best," and we arrived at the James's "refreshed,"—to use Miss Porter's word.

But the most celebrated walk through Chestertown was taken by Allen Ginsberg and his lover Peter Orlofsky, followed by a dozen or so Washington College student poets: a peripatetic Aristotelian stroll through the heart of town.

The night before, Ginsberg had given a reading in the Norman James Theatre (spelled with the "re" that Norman James preferred). The place was packed, mainly with students and faculty, but with many people from Chestertown as well. At the reading Ginsberg read some of his more famous poems: "Howl" ("the best minds of my generation have gone mad"), "Supermarket in California" ("What thoughts I have of you tonight Walt Whitman"), "America" ("I'm putting my queer shoulder to the wheel"), but Ginsberg also read for the first time his now celebrated poem "Mind Breath," a poem that in its story circles the globe, starting that first night at Washington College, Chestertown, Maryland, and traveling through the times zones of the Western United States, then on to Asia and Europe, to return to the podium from where he read. It was an astounding poem.

The next day Ginsberg and Peter Orlofsky sat on the steps of the Richmond House (the Literary House of those days) talking about poetry. I remember Orlofsky had a guitar on which he would strum now and then in some relationship with whatever Allen Ginsberg was saying; I suppose it was a kind of emphasis, but I could never figure out a pattern.

After about an hour of talking with the students, Ginsberg got up and asked me if we might walk the campus and then through town. He wanted to levitate some of the buildings—both on the campus and off. "Sure," I said. The dean had recently admonished the faculty to provide "unique educational experiences" for our students, and I thought a building levitation might look good on my annual report. "Engaged learning" we now call it.

"Levitate whatever you want," I said.

"Can we watch?" asked one student.

"I'll bet you can't levitate Reid Hall," said a woman with red hair.

Off we went, Ginsberg leading us with Orlofsky among the students strumming the guitar. Our first stop was the administration building, Bunting Hall.

With the students gathered behind them Ginsberg started a chant. "Ohmmmm. Ohmmmm. Ohmmmmmmmmmm." After a few moments when the building did not move, Ginsberg took small metal finger cymbals out of his pocket and, closing his eyes, rattled the cymbals and chanted with what seemed to me special vigor. "Ohmm! Ohmm! Ohmm!"

Still no movement of Bunting Hall.

"It is a very heavy building," said Ginsberg. "No doubt full of bureaucrats."

"Let's go downtown," I said. "They've been talking about moving the old jail from in front of the court house and maybe you can help them."

"Lead on," said Orlofsky.

So off we all went down Mount Vernon Avenue, then took a right at Kent Street, a left at Calvert past the post office ("Very heavy buildings," said Orlofsky) through the park then to the jail—which has since been moved to the edge of the town by the railroad tracks.

Ginsberg and Orlofsky looked at the jail for a moment. They left our group and went around to the side by Emmanuel Episcopal Church and looked at the jail from that angle. From where we were standing we could see they were in earnest conversation, no doubt discussing the best angle by which to raise the building—Orlofsky apparently wanting to pry it up from the side, but Ginsberg holding out for a full frontal floatation. They returned. By now a number of townspeople had gathered around our group.

"Where do they want it moved?" asked Ginsberg.

"I don't know," I said. "But I think they'd be grateful if you just got it off the ground because that would at least be a start."

"Jails are very heavy buildings," said Ginsberg. And then to Peter Olofsky he started a spontaneous poetic chant (accompanied by Orlofsky on his guitar) enumerating the various jails into which one or the other of them—or both—had been tossed over the years. It was a splendid chant, and I wondered then if someday I might not see it in print as a poem. By this time I noticed that some of the men who were in the jail on the second floor had come to the windows to see what was going on.

"Maybe Reid Hall would be easier," said the young lady with the red hair. But by that time the chanting and finger cymbals and the guitar were in full swing: "Ohmmmmm! Ohmmmmmm. Ohm! Ohm. Ohmmmmmmmmmmmmm!"

It didn't work. For half an hour it didn't work. No jail moved. Maybe a hundred "Ohmmmms!" The jail stayed on the ground. The inmates seemed disappointed.

But in the end it seemed not to matter that the buildings of Washington College and Chestertown could not be levitated. There was the story of them not moving. The story of the chanting. The story of the walk back through town as Ginsberg recited Whitman's poetry and his own, speaking a line of his, and then a line of Whitman's, weaving an American poem a hundred years old and twenty years old at once. These stories were levitation in their own way.

Years later a student wrote me to claim the jail had in fact been raised by all the "Ohmmmmms." He could see it in his mind's eye, hovering above the ground, then easing down Cross Street toward the train station. The men in the jail were cheering as they went, as if to be in the air was to be free. I wondered what my student had been smoking that day.

A Literary Luncheon Party

MARY WOOD

"WOULD YOU LIKE TO invite James Dickey to lunch, during his visit to Washington College?" asked Bob Day. It was the spring of 1972, before Dickey had been televised nationwide reading a poem at Jimmy Carter's inauguration but, after his novel *Deliverance* had become a best-seller. Bob mentioned *Buckdancer's Choice*, Dickey's acclaimed first book of poetry, and other honors, sparing me the shame of having to admit I'd never heard of the man.

We arranged that the luncheon would take place on the day after his evening reading. Bob wanted to include one or two writing students, one of whom, afterward, would drive Mr. Dickey to Friendship Airport.

Giddy with the reflected glory in which my bucolic social life was about to bask, I rushed to my tattered copy of Strand's *Anthology*, which had often rescued me from gaps in my knowledge of contemporary poetry.

I read the strange, strong, beautiful poems. "The Performance" was an elegy for an airman friend who liked to do handstands. He was captured by the Japanese, decapitated:

And the headsman broke down…
And if some other one had not told him,
Would have cut off the feet.

"Heaven for Animals" is another elegy. Some say this is an apology for hunting. I don't agree. It is about hope. Dickey holds his words just this side of sentimentality:

Here they are. Their soft eyes open.
If they have lived in wood,
It is a wood.
If they have lived on plains,
It is grass rolling
Under their feet forever.

The person who wrote these lines sitting at my table! How the conversation would sparkle. I then read *Deliverance*. A faint warning bell sounded in my head, but the canoeing scenes were splendid.

I invited my elegant friend Lynette Nielsen, who was on the board or about to be on the board of Washington College and who had heard of Dickey, also Bill Thompson '70, a winner of the Sophie Kerr Prize, who was working at the Centreville *Record-Observer*, and my husband. "I know you're not big on poetry, but this guy is one of the leading poets in our country today, and you have to eat somewhere, so you might as well come home." His law office is in Centreville, ten minutes from the farm. "All right," he said, polite and resigned, as he has often had to be with me.

Lynette and I drove up to the reading in Hynson Lounge the night before. Along with everyone else we waited and waited until a scuffling sound was heard, and up the aisle came Mr. Dickey herded by a phalanx of nervous members of the English faculty. They were helping to hold him up, I learned later. Nicholas Newlin, a gentleman from his old-school tie to polished shoes, was chairman of the department. He rose to introduce the speaker. I wish I could remember what he said. I am sure it was a gem of understatement, irony and vague alarm.

The poet rose, propped himself on the lectern, and slurred out an unattractive series of images having to do with adultery, a motel room, rumpled sheets, and then he sat down. There was a long silence. Five minutes, at most, had passed since his introduction. Dr Newlin looked at his watch. "Mr. Dickey, would you care to read some more?"

"No."

The next morning as I was bustling through last-minute hostess things, the telephone rang. It was Bob Day, sounding harassed. "Mary, you don't have to go through with it. He's been on a terrible tear." Figuring that something had to be done with the poet and his hangover until plane time, I said that they might as well bring him here.

My other guests arrived first. I briefed them on the latest developments. We sat and made polite, apprehensive chat. Then the college cars rolled up. There was some noise as my guests negotiated two steps, the screen door, the front door.

The eminent poet swayed in the doorway, arms holding the jams. He wore vaguely Western clothing, and his eyes looked like oysters. "Ah bi a bayud boy," he announced, aimed himself at the sofa, put his leather cowboy hat down over his eyes, and passed out.

In a whispered consolation, Bob and I hustled Danny Williams, the student driver, into the kitchen and dished him up a plate of food. Meanwhile, back in the living room sipping sherry, Sarah Gearhart, the other student, and the rest of us made light, though rather stiff conversation, whispering in order to keep the sleeping poet safe in the arms of Morpheus. When the driver had stoked up on enough food to sustain him through his coming ordeal, Bob approached the sofa.

"Well Mr. Dickey," he yelled in ringing tones, "Thank Mrs. Wood for the nice luncheon. It's time to catch your plane." With considerable hoisting, the poet was propped up on his feet and, as he stumbled out the door, tipped the cowboy hat and said politely, "Thank you ma'am. I had a real nice time." He was poured into the car and off they rode.

We sighed in relief, poured out another round of sherries and went into lunch. Bill Thompson says we ate shrimp salad, Sarah thinks chicken. Lynette has left us for Heaven for Artists, as has Dickey, but he wouldn't have known as he never had lunch, and I don't remember.

Just as we were ready to begin my husband arrived. "Sorry to be late," he said looking around the table, and asked, "Where's the poet?"

The Address Book

WILLIAM CHAPMAN BOWIE

1.
A College Reunion

"So, you still write?" she asks; meeting her eye
I grip my minor, classic tome,
Addresses, stashed in my suit coat pocket, and try
calling up a name to fit her face, which isn't
familiar either, although one time
at least, I guess, we must have met — *Sue*
or *Suzy?* A braid of frightening greys
edits her tag. "Well, yes, nice to see you
again." A partial lie. Then, as we've done
before, we go our separate ways
into rooms crowded with noise, while outside
across a sun-stopped scene of lawn,
striped tents, and bar-b-q's set up in the quad
(where, this afternoon, we're meant to gather
again and hear drag on and on
officialdom's own windy *Welcome Back*),
the translucent shadow of a cloud
drifts past, like that undoable magic trick
where, as the black cloth is pulled away,
we're startled to see nothing has changed.

2.
The Novel

Pigskin covers and marbled end-papers
dignify the costly rag, although it seems
I still rework it every couple of years.
Addresses remains the working title,
and love, travel, and time its ancient themes.
But it's modern enough, with its exposition
cleanly hidden between the lines, and that
cast of characters I've written in
and written out, often dissatisfied,
oddly, as much by those I haven't met
as by those I have — one part graphite,
the ones who came to star for a scene
or two and then get written out;
and one part, friends, the ones who settled down
in epic migrations from pencil to pen.

Women's Work: Forging a Town's Character

MARCIA C. LANDSKROENER

> "Woman as a factor in town improvement has been a brilliant success in Chestertown. She has done in three years what the men of Chestertown would not have accomplished in three centuries."
> — Fred G. Usilton in the *History of Kent County, Maryland, 1630-1916*

WHEN THE FIRST SCHOONERS carrying settlers landed at the Port of Chester 300 years ago, the division of labor between genders was fairly predictable. The men went fishing and hunting, tilled the land and started businesses. The women were caregivers, predominantly wives and homemakers bound by the rules of a patriarchal society to play second fiddle to their men. Our colonial mothers no doubt wielded subtle power on the home front—whether to raise sheep or pigs, where to put the outhouse, when to plant the tomatoes. They surely bore the responsibility for the gardens and children, beating carpets, doing laundry, polishing floors. Unless they could afford domestic help, the lives of these women barely changed until the early 1900s, when electric appliances eased the burden of keeping house. But when by necessity those domestic bounds were stretched—when husbands died, when fortunes changed—or when independent-minded women rebelled against social convention and refused to marry, Chestertown's women demonstrated just how strong and resourceful and influential they could be. Today, Chestertown is brimming with independent women—business owners, educators, political and community leaders, writers, artists, scientists, community planners and others. These women are in debt to their sisters who came before.

My great-grandmother Lillie Viola Hadaway—the oldest person I ever knew—is long dead, having passed away at the age of 99, some 30 years ago, from apparent boredom. She never went beyond her front gate, choosing instead to hear of the world from family and friends, including deaf old Sally Crosby, the Rock Hall stringer for one of the Chestertown newspapers who gathered her news through an ear trumpet. But Lillie was of Rock Hall stock, and certifiably agoraphobic, not like those Chestertown suffragettes who were comfortable moving from place to place—women like her own daughter, Daisy, a Riveting Rosie who assembled airplanes in Baltimore during World War II. If Lillie were alive, she would tell me stories of other women who in years past stepped outside the bounds of convention. Women who have changed the very fabric of our community. But then, she didn't gossip much.

For that, I had to go to Chestertown.

I called upon the oldest, and smartest, women I knew for wisdom and guidance, including my mother. And I got an earful. It seems that if it weren't for women's work, Chestertown would be a different place altogether. It would be dirty and smelly, sure. But it would also be a place without schools and libraries and parks. A place without beauty, or community spirit, or revolutionary ideas. Apparently, women of Chestertown have always had a knack for what business leaders today call "continuous improvement." The ladies of Chestertown see a need, and set out to fill it. And they often accomplished great things.

My great-grandmother Lillie's best friend was Nellie Schreiber, who moved from Rock Hall to Chestertown. The Schreibers had a store at 337 High Street in Chestertown. Their name is still on the building, and one of their two daughters, Miss Carrie, still holds court from her home on High Street. Funny thing about those Schreiber girls: Neither Carrie nor Ada married.

"We dated boys in our day," Miss Carrie says, "but we never felt we needed to get married to get along. And no one ever looked at us any differently."

Miss Ada worked as a secretary for an insurance company, and later helped her father run the store, which sold newspapers and magazines, candy and tobacco. But like most women of Chestertown, she did what she could to enliven this small town. Miss Ada was instrumental in establishing a local chapter of the Order of the Eastern Star, a charitable organization that perpetuates Christian ideals while giving women a reason to get dressed up for Tuesday night meetings. Miss Ada was the first worthy matron of the Chestertown Chapter #86 OES, and remained active throughout her life.

After graduating from high school in 1934, her sister Carrie, at their father's insistence, studied at Washington College before launching a career in education that would last 49 years. Miss Carrie always knew she would become a school teacher but, when she graduated in 1938, with the Great Depression still in swing, she says "school teachers were a dime a dozen." It was women's work, and thus low pay. But education was a field in which women could wield their influence. There were very few jobs for young people in Chestertown, so she and her friends all went to Baltimore looking for work. Miss Carrie spent much of her teaching career away from Chestertown, returning in 1973 to finish at Kent School.

Back in the 1930s and 1940s, Miss Carrie recalls, there were a few female business owners: Miss Hannah and Miss Margaret Bell ran the Bellehaven, a tearoom and boarding house located in what is now the Rose O'Neill Literary House on the Washington College campus. At one time, college boys lived in the rooms upstairs, but the tearoom was open to all. The Bellehaven was renowned for its wonderful food, much of it prepared by the black ladies who would be collected every morning from their homes on Langford Road. Miss Hannah made the fancy desserts, the icebox cake and lemon meringue pies, while her cousin Margaret ran the tearoom.

There were other, more formidable female presences in Chestertown. Miss Harriett Welch, a lifelong resident of Queen Street, began teaching when her father became ill. She operated her own kindergarten for 25 years, starting in the Sophie Fisher House with twelve children. When the Foxes moved to town in the early 1930s, Mrs. Baurice Fox worked side-by-side with her husband at Fox's Five and Dime. Miss Dorothy Paca was a woman of exquisite taste who offered the latest women's fashions at Paca's Dress Shop in the 1940s and '50s. Jane Cooper worked as a pharmacist at Stam's Drug Store in the 1920s and '30s. She had her full degree, while Miss Hallie Toulson became a druggist at her father's store through an apprenticeship. Joan Horsey's mother, Kitty Ozman, was Chestertown's first female magistrate, or Justice of the Peace—the first stop between the scene of the crime and the jail-house. But there was no more formidable presence, to the youngsters of Chestertown Elementary School at least, than Miss Marietta Loud. As a seventh-grade teacher and school principal, Miss Loud was adored, feared and respected.

Yet even before then, Miss Carrie assured me, women had been at work shaping the character of the town of Chestertown through their civic activities. In 1898, the women of Chestertown planted a garden.

FOUNTAIN PARK

The Town Improvement Society was formed in July 1898, with Mrs. Thomas W. Eliason as its president, with Mrs. George B. McWhorter, Mrs. James Brice, Mrs. James A. Pearce, Mrs. William J. Vannort and Mrs. Eben F. Perkins as vice presidents, and with Mrs. Wilbur W. Hubbard, among others, on the Executive Committee. According to the History of Chestertown, the society was "composed of ladies, whose purpose it [was] to beautify the public squares of Chestertown and advance the town from an aesthetic point of view."

An old market house had been in operation on that square of land, and had fallen on hard times. It was smelly and ill kept. The ladies decided to clean up the lot and erect a fountain at its center. Mrs. Hubbard sent her husband to the Robert Wood Foundry in Philadelphia to purchase the ornate fountain, which is crowned by a statue of Hebe,

Goddess of Youth and Beauty and Cupbearer to the Gods. The fountain was delivered by rail to the station at the head of High Street. From there, a horse-drawn wagon lumbered the fountain to its present site.

The women designed the brick walkways, based on a plate in Mrs. Hubbard's china cupboard, and planted shrubbery, trees and flowers. Today, members of the Chestertown Garden Club, a successor to the Town Improvement Society, are responsible for the upkeep of Fountain Park, as well as the town's seasonal finery.

I know it's Christmas in Chestertown when Hebe takes on her mantle of green and every lamppost in the park sprouts magnolia leaves, holly sprigs and ribbons. While other towns throughout the Eastern Shore favor gaudy tinsel and plastic candy canes hanging from their streetlights, Chestertown glows with a natural beauty—a reflection, no doubt, of its Garden Club membership, natural beauties all.

In 2006 the Chestertown Garden Club celebrates its seventy-fifth birthday. The legacy of the Town Improvement Society is much in evidence at every Saturday morning Farmers' Market, on warm summer evenings during Music in the Park, at every Chestertown Tea Party, and at the Club's annual May Mart. Townspeople and visitors alike are drawn to the heart of this town where the voices of Chestertown's women whisper through the peonies.

Recently, the Garden Club ladies have turned their attention to another park—Wilmer Park—where they are undertaking an ambitious tidal marsh restoration project along the shoreline. The cattails of my youth have been nearly choked out of existence by some invasive species, and I'm not talking about land developers from Philadelphia. If anyone can eradicate the plague of phragmites and return a natural beauty to the wetlands of Chestertown with native sedges and reeds, it's her gentle female gardeners.

CHESTERTOWN'S MATRIARCH

Perhaps one of the most outspoken women in Chestertown was Mrs. Wilbur W. Hubbard, mother of the famed master of foxhounds, Wilbur

Ross Hubbard. In 1919, Mrs. Hubbard was recognized in the Baltimore *American* newspaper as one "who impressed upon us the necessity of conservation, of patriotic sacrifice, of unity of service; who inspired us to greater achievement as only loyal, devoted women can do."

Etta Belle Ross Hubbard was active in the Woman's National Democratic Club, highly educated, and well informed politically. She spent every winter in Washington, traveling in political circles, and served a term as president of the national organization.

In the days when a college education for young ladies was unusual, Mrs. Hubbard sent her own daughter to Paris for schooling. She penned several political treatises, including *The A.B.C. of Jefferson and Hamilton*—written in support of President Roosevelt's economic policies to put people back to work. "Why can't businessmen see that capital, labor, farmer and consumer are all dependent each upon the other for success and that their hearts as well as their heads must go into business?" she wrote. "This is the Roosevelt system—raise wages, shorten hours, and lower the price of your product. This system will give farmers and laborers, 90 percent of your people, money to buy the things they want and they want everything, and your factories will run twenty-four hours with three shifts a day to supply the things they want."

During World War II, she wrote a pamphlet titled *No Dictator Shall Snatch Tomorrow From The Eternal Will.* "Shall we the people of America who have sacrificed and given so willingly, go back to the old selfish life or shall we fulfill our Destiny by establishing a new and better order for ourselves and set an example for the world?" Here, Mrs. Hubbard proposed that the government provide interest-free credit to returning war veterans, permitting them to build homes, purchase farmland and start up businesses and factories. This, she declared, would assure the nation's economic stability and the preservation of the family.

But perhaps the most remarkable thing about Mrs. Hubbard was her work as a historic preservationist, conducted long before anyone really understood the value and significance of preserving examples of America's earliest architecture. She was an historical purist who directed teams of workmen to conserve antique paneling and woodwork, rather than replace original elements with modern fixtures. When in 1910 she and her husband purchased Widehall, one of the most historically significant structures in Chestertown, she transformed it into a showcase. A decade later, she directed that an entire house be moved from Massachusetts to Washington, DC, where she had it restored to its original condition.

According to Mackey Dutton, if the men of Chestertown had listened to Mrs. Hubbard, the town today would have several colonial gems that have since been lost to male pride and the march of progress. Mrs. Hubbard went to the board of the Chestertown Bank of Maryland (Mackey's uncle, Scott Beck, was the bank president at the time) and begged them not to tear down the original building next to Stam's Drug Store on High Street. But they ignored her and built what many considered "a grey monolith, a modern monstrosity."

Built in 1929, the Chestertown Bank of Maryland structure was inspired by the classical architecture of Greece. According to historic preservationist Marsha Fritz, its large columns and grand lobby are symbols of stability. (Ironically, the building was completed just before the American economy collapsed.) Fritz suspects that the board wanted to replace the colonial structure with a larger, more impressive structure that would also provide better functionality for the business of banking. From her perspective, "it's a wonderful piece of architecture. The details, materials and execution are superb," she says, "and it still works. I can understand Mrs. Hubbard's position, and I may have felt the same way at the time. Too bad there couldn't be a way to have both."

As part of the Historical Society of Kent County's oral history project conducted in the 1980s, Wilbur Hubbard talked about his mother. "She was a very unusual woman," he recalls. "She was just way ahead of her time." Soon after the family purchased Widehall, Mrs. Hubbard devoted all of her energies to restoring the colonial mansion to its original splendor, and filling it with period antiques.

"She spent a great deal of her time arguing with my father and the architect," Wilbur recalled. "My father just wanted to pay the bill and get the whole damn thing over with, and the architect wanted to do too much. He knew something about colonial woodwork and mouldings and so forth, but he wanted to dress it up and show how much he knew, and mother kept saying 'no, I want to put it back as nearly as possible to the way it was originally.' Well, that's modern restoration. Nobody was doing that in 1910, 1911, and the ladies up and down Water just didn't understand mother," he said. "After she got through [with the restoration] she went around buying antique furniture, and they said, 'Just imagine, Mrs. Hubbard spending all that money to fix over that old house when she could have built a new one, and for less. And now she's going around buying second-hand furniture to put in it."

Not everything in the Hubbard household was antique. The Hubbards had the first telephone in Chestertown—as early as 1916. Mrs. Hubbard apparently had a lot to say on any number of subjects.

Of Roy Kirby's recent restoration of Widehall, I'm sure she would have nothing but praise: "Finally, a man who got it right."

BLACK HANDS: LABORING ON EARTH AND PRAYING FOR REWARD IN HEAVEN

Chestertown has been a racially divided community throughout its 300-year history. Right about the time that Mrs. Hubbard was busy restoring her mansion, a baby girl was born to an African-American family in Big Woods. She was one of 23 children, ten of whom survived.

As a young girl, Delia Ringgold Caulk worked in the fields, did domestic work, and worked for several canneries. At hog butchering time, she went from farm to farm, where she helped cut up meat, made scrapple, and put up lard in 50-pound cans. She later worked at the Rigbie Hotel in Betterton, where as a "pantry girl" she washed and sorted the silver for each waitress. She worked at the Chestertown Cannery and the Vita Foods plant. At one time, she was the only black woman who worked at the old Acme store, where she dressed chickens. Even later, she cleaned several Washington College facilities, including Minta Martin Hall and the Hynson-Ringgold House, where she worked for President and Mrs. Daniel Gibson.

Yet apart from her lifetime of labor, Mrs. Caulk served the Lord and her community. She was the first president of the No. 2 Kent and Queen Anne's Hospital Auxiliary (No. 2 indicating the black membership), and at one time she was chaplain of the Kent County PTA. Her life centered around Fountain Methodist Church on Big Woods Road, where the pastor and parishioners called her "Old Faithful" and "Rock of Gibraltar" because they could always count on her to help. She taught Sunday school, and was president of what is now the Methodist Women. At one time she was in a "praying band," part of a troupe of musicians with only their voices for instruments.

According to the oral history collection at the Historical Society of Kent County, "Mrs. Caulk was always a Republican as most colored people were, but she always prayed for both parties."

Were her prayers ever answered? I'd like to think so, now that Chestertown is nearly color-blind. I know mine were. My working-class family was not the kind that could afford domestic help—that's what daughters were for, my mother reminded me, as I practiced my ironing on pillowcases and handkerchiefs—but I was fascinated by the world of those more privileged mothers and daughters who sent their ironing out; mothers and daughters who hired strong, capable hands from Big Woods to help in the kitchen, to dust and vacuum their spacious waterfront homes. It was the work of women like Mrs. Caulk who eased the domestic burden of Chestertown's middle- and upper-class women but, personally, I will always be thankful for the advent of permanent press fabric. Thank you, Jesus.

FEMALE PERSUASION: ARGUING FOR COEDUCATION AT
WASHINGTON COLLEGE

On the Washington College campus today, female students outnumber their male counterparts three to two. For some reason, women typically are the stronger academic performers, more driven to succeed. They try harder, perhaps because they understand their great-great-grand-mothers had to talk their way into the classroom and prove themselves worthy of a college education.

According to college lore, it happened one warm day in early September 1891, when a group of young local ladies on an excursion from Chestertown to Baltimore found a captive audience in Professor Proctor. Proctor taught biology and chemistry at Washington College, and often took the steamer to Baltimore to visit relatives. During the ride across the bay, the exchange, as reported by Sue DePasquale in the Fall 1991 issue of the *Washington College Magazine*, went like this:

"Jarred from his reveries by the rustle of petticoats, he opened one eye to see a band of young women clustered about.

"'Did he teach at Washington College?' they inquired. 'Why, yes,' Proctor responded pleasantly. Their next question was not as easy: 'Why aren't women allowed to attend classes at the college?' Proctor had no ready answer. He knew the college's charter did not deny them the opportunity. Yet up to now, Washington College, like many other colleges of the day, was the unchallenged realm of the 'stronger' sex. (Gettysburg College had enrolled its first women only six years earlier. The College of William and Mary would not follow suit until 1918.)

"Sensing the professor's hesitation, the young women jumped in with a friendly barrage of reasons as to why they should be able to enroll at Washington College. They were sincere, their arguments well executed, and Proctor found he was warming to their cause. He promised to take their case before College president Charles Reid.

"Reid, too, was easily won over. On September 18, 1891, he proposed to the Board of Visitors and Governors that females be admitted to classes and lectures as day students. The Board adopted the resolution (mostly for pecuniary reasons, historians speculate today), and the first eleven young women became members of the student body of Washington College."

Two years later, the College would hire its first female faculty member. Miss Bertha M. Stiles taught English, mathematics and German. She also became the College's first housemother, when Normal Hall opened in the spring of 1897. By establishing a Normal Department to train women as public school teachers, the College was able to qualify for

State funding for the construction of the female dormitory, known today as Reid Hall.

The majority of female students enrolled at that time opted to take the two-year Normal Course. By the spring of 1911, the College had awarded normal certificates to 132 women. By contrast, only fourteen women had earned bachelor's degrees.

These numbers gave college administrators pause. Fearing the College's liberal arts mission was being overshadowed by the teaching program, and citing the "disciplinary problem" of housing men and women on the same campus, the College terminated the Normal Department that year and closed Normal Hall, accepting women only as day students enrolled in the academic program. In 1919, after women had won the right to vote, the Board of Visitors reconsidered women's rights to an equal education and reopened the women's dormitory for boarding students. Normal Hall was enlarged and renamed to honor the College president who had first opened the doors of Washington College to women. One of those early female pioneers would return to receive an honorary doctoral degree for her achievements in the field of education. But first, she started a book club.

THE WOMEN'S LITERARY CLUB

On December 2, 1902, a group of women came together under the direction of Mary Adele France to establish a Women's Literary Club. By 1907, the women had opened the town's first library.

Miss France, who was born in Quaker Neck in 1878, graduated from Washington College in 1900, nine years after the College had opened its doors to women. After teaching assignments in Kentucky and in Washington, DC, she became president of St. Mary's Female Seminary (now St. Mary's College of Maryland). In recognition of her contributions to education, Washington College awarded Miss France the honorary degree of Doctor of Letters in 1942, during the same ceremony at which two other women, Sophie Kerr and Eleanor Roosevelt, were honored. Addie France was just twenty-four when she launched her book club.

The Women's Literary Club brought literary-minded ladies together for the purpose of reading and sharing books. According to Mrs. Ella Robinson, who in 1957 wrote an account of the Library's fifty-year history, the Library received a large collection of books when the "Young Men's Club" disbanded and apparently lost interest in reading the books that had been donated to them by certain townspeople. The women formed a Library Board chosen from the membership of the Club.

Among the charter members of the Women's Literary Club were Susiebelle Culp, Mary Cacy Burchinal, Hallie Isabel Toulson (our druggist), Mabel Toulson, Hallie Roberts Westcott, Irma Briscoe Eliason, Ann Burton Smith, Julia Merrit Burchinal, Antoiniette Louise Stam and Rebecca Brown Watson.

The Library's first home was on the second floor of the old Bank of Chestertown. It was later housed above the offices of the Mutual Fire Insurance Company, before the ladies negotiated purchase in 1943 of the building on the corner of High and Queen Streets. Through the years, the Women's Literary Club financed the public library through various fundraisers—"Old Chestertown Days," antiques shows, hobby shows, card parties, movie benefits, the sale of Christmas cards—and personal donations.

Miss Fannie Stuart provided a gift in memory of her sister, Sarah Elizabeth Stuart, to organize and maintain a children's room. Miss Anne B. Smith provided generously for the Chestertown Public Library in her will. The library's collection had grown over the years to include more than 20,000 volumes of fiction, nonfiction, reference and children's collections. In 1966, the Library circulated more than 12,750 books to 5,750 patrons.

The first librarian was Miss Josephine Wheatley, followed by Miss Polly Westcott, Miss Blanche Constable, Miss Emily Ford Baker and Miss Nellie Walters. But most people today remember Miss Cornelia "Neelie" Davis, who filled the post for more than forty years, with the help of her dear companion, Miss Dorothy Paca. My mother-in-law was among the paying Chestertown Library patrons who adored Neelie. As a youngster, I got my reading material from the Bookmobile that parked behind Rock Hall High School every Wednesday, but I remember Cornelia Davis from

Christmas Eve services at Old St Paul's. As she went to take communion, the little bells she had sewn on her knee socks jingled merrily.

Miss Davis tragically took her own life on the steps of the Kent County Courthouse. Was her final act a statement of personal loss or social commentary? Was Chestertown too cruel a place for unmarried women? Was the weight of her rebellion against society's norms too much to bear? Was the Chestertown Library too small a refuge from the mean-spiritedness of the world? How far have we come since the publication of Kate Chopin's *The Awakening,* really? There is only so much comfort one can take in books. I suspect the Chestertown Library was as much about friendships as it was about reading.

When the Kent County Public Library was built in 1978, use of the little private library on the corner declined. Sadly, the Chestertown Library closed its doors in 2001, and Washington College incorporated many Chestertown Library books into its own collection. Today, Chestertown women are still big readers, and still enjoy their monthly book clubs. But I don't know of another soul who wears jingle bells to Christmas Eve services.

PROMOTING A HEALTHY COMMUNITY

In 1934, the brand new Chestertown Hospital consisted of a doctor's office and operation room, four private rooms, men's and women's wards and an x-ray department. Dr. A.C. Dick would soon take up residence in the office, but the opening of the hospital presented new career opportunities for the women of Chestertown. With Dr. Dick's arrival in 1935, he encouraged many to go for their nurse's training at Union Memorial Hospital in Baltimore, where he had launched his career. Thus began a long line of women who helped deliver babies, assisted during surgeries, and provided patient care in a modern health care facility.

Florence Skirven Corey was the first director of nursing at the hospital. Sarah Strong, Catherine Short and Maryland Massey, who graduated from Washington College in 1968, followed in her footsteps.

"Miss Flossie was the most caring person," Massey recalls. "Everybody loved her. She was real calm and gracious—with a certain posture that brought comfort to her patients."

Mary Louise "Mal" Watson, who worked at the hospital for nearly forty years, remembers working under Florence in the early 1950s. "There are lots of stories about Florence," Mrs. Watson says. "She was all about 'making do.' She would go around with aspirins in one pocket and sleeping pills in the other, and as an young nurse just out of Union Memorial I gasped," she laughs. "And I still chuckle to remember the man who asked Florence for a towel for his sponge bath. 'You don't need a towel,' she says. 'Just stand there in front of that fan and you'll dry off.'"

In those early years, maternity patients had to walk up the stairs before delivering their babies. There was one delivery room, and one nurse and one aide on every shift. Maryland Massey has an indelible image of Harriet Oliffe in the nursery. "She was the mother of all mothers," Massey says. "She had a big bosom, and she would prop those babies on her chest one after the other and feed them every night."

Miss Florence remained a presence at the hospital even after she retired. She would carry a basket of goodies down the hall, doling out cheerful little gifts to patients and nursing staff alike—African violets, cookies, pens, even cooking utensils. In that volunteer role, she was the forerunner of the Hospital Auxiliary, a group of women dedicated to supporting the hospital through volunteer staffing and with its various fundraising efforts. To benefit the hospital, the Auxiliary operates the hospital's gift shop, runs the Nearly New thrift shop (Miss Florence's favorite store), and sponsors the annual Christmas Shop, now in its thirty-eighth year. In 1958, Mrs. Watson became a charter member of the organization that today provides 130 volunteer hours a week. Since its inception, the Christmas Shop alone has raised nearly $900,000 for hospital projects.

Yet long before the hospital was built, women were caring for the sick. For nearly fifty years, one woman in particular was an angel of mercy to those in the Chestertown community who, without her, would have had little or no access to health care. Highly educated and motivated to improve the lives of the poor and underserved populations, Marjorie Hawkins was a treasured resource within the black community and a well-respected presence in her field. While she couldn't go out to lunch in Chestertown with her white colleagues, she had crossed certain racial boundaries long before the Civil Rights movement.

Originally from Chicago, young Marjorie Forte was working in Chestertown as early as 1926. She was the first black public health nurse in Kent County, perhaps in the State of Maryland. She later married Elmer T. "Hap" Hawkins, who served for many years as principal of Garnett High School. At the time, he was the only high school principal in the county with a doctorate, and Garnett flourished under his steady hand. In all likelihood, his wife had helped to deliver many of the children under his care.

In the first half of the 20th century, public health nurses did it all: home visits, childhood immunizations, prenatal care, health education, counseling, social services advocacy and midwifery, in addition to assisting with clinics during the periodic visits of physicians from Baltimore. In the 1920s, Marjorie Hawkins worked out of an office on High Street with Mrs. Don Falls, assisting the ear, nose and throat specialist who came to Chestertown one day a week. She also worked with visiting obstetricians. But for routine medical care, Mrs. Hawkins was on the front lines, doing what she could to prevent and treat illnesses, and deliver healthy babies. She worked closely with Kent County's sanitation officer, Mr. Rollison McGinnis, to insure that black families with shallow wells and/or failing septic systems had safe drinking water. And she was a public health educator. Not only was she a skilled and practiced midwife, but she trained the five midwives who worked under her, as well as several registered nurses from developing countries who spent two months in Kent County in the late 1940s/early 1950s learning the trade from Mrs. Hawkins.

In 1930, she went to Detroit during National Negro Health Week to receive the Rural Community Prize, a silver cup recognizing her contributions. In 1943, she attended a conference on providing services for Negro children, sponsored by the U.S. Department of Labor's Children's Bureau. In 1943-44, she completed a six-month course in nurse/midwifery at Tuskegee Institute. Three decades later, she was still delivering babies, black and white, and caring for patients who came to the Kent County Health Department. A lot of mothers wouldn't let anyone but Marjorie Hawkins administer immunization shots to their children.

Anne Newsome worked as a secretary at the health department while Mrs. Hawkins was there. "She had a very professional demeanor and didn't discuss her patients," Newsome recalls, "but Marjorie had some heartaches. I remember her almost crying when a young girl came in, not quite twelve, and pregnant. She said, 'I've worked all my life to keep this from happening, and it's still happening.' She took care of all her pregnant girls. If she had a difficult case she would transfer them to the hospital, but there were only six or eight doctors in Kent County at the time I went to work in 1949."

Many of the patients Mrs. Hawkins saw didn't have the money, or the insurance, to pay those doctors.

"She visited some very poor houses—rental properties where environmental problems had existed for years," Mr. McGinnis recalls. "Sometimes we made visits together, and suggested things the families could do without much money, like boiling water. She came to Chestertown at a time when local people didn't have doctors, when poor people didn't go to see doctors. She was the person they relied upon. When she retired [in 1973], all of Chestertown's business and community leaders came to honor her for all she had accomplished under what were sometimes very difficult conditions. As a black person she wasn't openly accepted at first, but she earned her place in the community and was well-respected when she left."

CHESTERTOWN HASN'T ALWAYS been fair to women, regardless of the color of their skin. We are somehow expected to do more with fewer resources: to find a way to bring about positive change using our creativity, our faith and our powers of persuasion, even if there's no money. We call upon our female friends, who sustain and encourage us. Had we consistently failed in our endeavors, perhaps the expectations and the demands society places upon us would fade. But the women's stories told here demonstrate what I've come to understand about this town of talented and resourceful women: we possess a certain inner strength that counterbalances any social impediments and compels us to do good work, not for financial gain but for the personal satisfaction that comes with forging a community we're proud to call home. Whether beautifying and preserving our environs, seeking better educational opportunities, improving access to health care, or reaching out to those in need—the women of Chestertown have shaped our fair town into a cohesive, literate, historically significant, and politically and culturally active community—a gem of the Eastern Seaboard.

River

JAMES DISSETTE

Finally I come to you again

simple as the Doctor's red wheel barrow
you are a slinking gouge

not smooth as a worn opera glove
not explaining the predicament of time
to the thieves who weep into your shallows
or the children who break you into diamonds

nor the silver covenant reflecting the faces of lovers
or the salt lick for the moon's curved tongue
or the wound where the soul slips its envelope of sorrows

but a dark wet heaven
for the spirits of cars, wedding rings,
the palms of slaves drifting like maple leaves,
fishhooks and chain, broken oars, urine, root and seed~

No matter how simple I try to keep you
    spring water gone brown still flowing to the bay

I come to you
and the jittery old cinemas crackle
on their sprockets and play
the voices of those I stood with on this bridge
their faces rise out of you
into the salt of my blood
rise with the moon laying
down its white history
rise to my throat and lips
until I must breath a song
to keep from drowning.

The Cheese Sandwich that Changed My Life

P. TRAMS HOLLINGSWORTH

LOTS OF SMALL DECISIONS have added up to big changes in my life. Truthfully these were more like wild whims than small decisions. Decisions denote some contemplation of actions and consequences. This, on the other hand, is the story of the one cheese sandwich that changed everything for me.

I chose to attend Washington College in the town of Chestertown on Maryland's Eastern Shore. Sort of. I was a senior at the Gunston School in Centreville, Maryland. Gunston in those days was a girls' boarding school where the student body, seventy teenagers, wore uniforms, and weekends spent in the wide world were in inverse proportion to the number of demerits piled up through each week. I hadn't been off-campus for a while when Mrs. Hoffecker, the school librarian, announced that she was loading the school bus for a trip to see the new movie *Butch Cassidy and the Sundance Kid.* "Bus fare" for senior students was one completed college application. It's not like I hadn't looked into college possibilities. I applied to Washington College because Paul Newman's son, Scott, was in attendance.

Four years later, under the Washington College Elm, I was front and center, capped and gowned, grinning as my mom posed the family photos. It was then, I remember clearly, that my father asked, "And what career do you intend to pursue with your now-documented insights into Romantic poetry?" Now when I think back upon that moment, I suspect that he was smirking. But I didn't see it then. I was stunned. I really hadn't thought of the future at all. I had daydreamed it in details. Sometimes I saw myself riding on the handlebars of Paul Newman's bike in the idyllic times between bank robberies. More often I saw myself poolside in some tropical paradise with Paul McCartney as he strummed and scribbled another one of the love songs inspired by our friendship. I just hadn't worked out the from-here-to-there stuff. And there under the Elm I was surprised to learn that my parents were not inclined to support me—financially speaking—as I mapped things out.

I waited tables, pumped some gas, and then I got lucky. The town of Chestertown was awarded funds from the Community Employment and Training Act (CETA) to hire some local underachievers for career assistance, and I was, no surprise, a candidate for application. Elmer Horsey was the mayor, and Billy Nicholson was the Town Manager. Bill Ingersoll was the director of Planning and Zoning, and he became my immediate supervisor. He taught me the skills I needed to help with the maintenance of the Town's new public housing project and to build picnic tables and benches for the Town park. I had one lesson in driving a bulldozer but that didn't go well. More often I drove a small grass-mowing tractor around the Town graveyard. I liked that. I would put my Diet Coke atop one headstone, my baby oil on another and my Sun-In on another and then swig, slather and squirt as my life went around in circles. I was happy knowing that I was ready to be noticed and carried away when Paul McCartney came through Chestertown.

One day in Summer 1981, on a break in the Town Office, I picked up a cup of coffee and the Baltimore *Sun* newspaper and read that Paul McCartney was recording on a tiny island called Montserrat in the British West Indies. On a whim, like so many before and after, I took a piece of the Mayor's gold embossed stationery and wrote a letter explaining why I should be hired to assist the care and entertainment of rock stars in the Caribbean. I sent letters to the two people mentioned in the article: George Martin, who had been the Beatles' producer, and

Skip Fraczek, the nightclub owner who was renting his villa to the McCartney family. Then I went back to cutting grass.

WEEKS LATER, an overseas telephone operator announced a call from Skip Fraczek on Montserrat; I assumed it was a joke until I heard the voice on the static-filled line asking if I would manage his nightclub while he returned to the States on personal business. He said he would put me up in his villa—occupied as we spoke by Paul McCartney and Stevie Wonder, show me the ropes of the bar business, and then be off for a short time while I sunbathed and supervised his operation. He wanted me there in two weeks.

When my small plane landed on the volcanic island at dusk, Skip was at the garage-sized terminal to meet me. The McCartneys, he explained, had left for London that morning, and he must also fly out sooner than anticipated. He would be returning to the States in the morning, but I could call him long distance if I had any questions—like, say, how to manage a villa and nightclub when I had never managed anything in my life.

Skip's villa was grander than I expected. His nightclub was not. Skip had told me that the locals showed up for rum and pizza in the afternoon, Canadian and American expatriates came to the club after dinner for beer and reggae, and often, after midnight, rock stars who were recording at Martin's nearby Air Studios would pile in for cognac and play music with the house band. But when I took my first self-guided tour of the club, it was as quiet as the graveyard I had left behind. The "nightclub" turned out to be a pavilion built of louvered shutters, which opened onto a black volcanic-sand beach. Fronds of banana and palm trees grew through the lattice back. Folding chairs were drawn up to rough-hewn tables. In the center of each sticky table, day-old oleander and hibiscus blossoms drooped from empty hot sauce-bottle vases.

Again, I had not really thought through the from-here-to-there and there-to-here stuff. But there were now thousands of miles between there, my home and my friends in Chestertown, and here, the tiny island I didn't know, where nobody knew me. The Montserratian staff had not yet arrived to sweep up last night's cigarette butts or to meet me, their new boss. The steady rain that drummed on the tin roof and splashed onto the cement floor made me feel every bit as alone as I really was.

I remember I was standing in the Club's kitchen, looking through the screen door, through the rain, down the pot-holed one-lane road, when I first laid eyes on the small boy picking through a trash can behind the rum shop next door. The boy had big bare feet and spindly legs with scabby knees showing below dirty shorts and a wet, too-small t-shirt stuck to his skinny chest and arms. Undeterred by my presence, he made his way toward the trash can just outside my kitchen door. Then from the other side of the screen he looked up and smiled at me as though he were an expected guest arriving for the luncheon that would be served from this dumpster. So I invited him into the kitchen, and we shared a sandwich I cobbled together from pizza ingredients. It didn't seem like a big deal at the time. Now, years later, I think of it as the cheese sandwich that changed my life.

The boy introduced himself as "LLLLLLenox Barzey." He stuttered through most sentences but L's were the hardest, and he often had to stamp his foot to get them out. We were still at the kitchen counter, chattering and stomping, when the club staff arrived later that afternoon. Everybody knew Lenox. Accepting me as Lenox's new friend, they began to coach me in my responsibilities as their supervisor. My chief duty, it seemed, was to keep a financial account of the operation, and to take the checkbook wherever it was needed. I shopped for supplies in the afternoon before opening, and I paid the band in the early morning after closing. I learned many things by trial and error. I learned that though plantains may look like bananas, the plantain daiquiri is not a popular drink, and that Rastafarian musicians named Kitaka and Ikim prefer not to be called by their checkbook names of Clarence and Dwight. I spent many days at Air Studios drinking champagne in the company of some very rich and very funny men as they reworked the lyrics of songs that the rest of the world had not yet heard. I was quite confident that I had, at last, found my life's work.

I also found that seven-year-old Lenox became a constant companion on my errands around his island. When I walked barefoot down the

PHOTO MARS GIBSON

In this 1986 photo, a ten-year-old Lenox Trams demonstrates the agility and charm that captured the heart of his adoptive mother.

road to market for laundry soap or to meet a rock star for lunch, I would look back and there would be Lenox, "walking" behind me on his hands, the pale pink soles of his dirty black feet pointed straight up at the sun. Then he'd tumble into cartwheels around me, race ahead, and wait for me to catch up. His front baby teeth had dropped out, so he had a big toothless grin that spread across his face and crowded the bright eyes that seemed to take in everything. I enjoyed Lenox's company and the attentions of cruising tourists and musicians who followed my acrobatic friend as he followed me. I enjoyed the friendships that grew as Lenox introduced me to the Montserratians and expatriates who had small businesses and few cares on the slow-moving island.

Lenox's mother, I learned, had been killed by a car when he was a baby. His father, a man whose street name was Sam Hustler, had a large legitimate family living in a nearby village. He acknowledged Lenox as his son but assumed no responsibility for this illegitimate child. Lenox shuttled among his mother's relatives: women he called Nanna and Auntie this and that, who lived with their extended families in one-room wooden houses on the beach or the mountainside. But really he lived on the streets and supported himself with his wits.

These were well honed. Once, when Lenox followed me into another restaurant in town, he pointed at the only pinball machine on the island

and asked, "How does it work?" I explained how, gave him a quarter and showed him how to start the machine up. He seemed reluctant. I assumed he wanted to keep the quarter for a worthier purchase. So I dropped my own quarter into the slot. When the machine exploded into action, I could read the reason for his hesitation. On the screen in front of us, the game's all-time high-scorer was announced in lights: Lenox Barzey. The champ gave me a sheepish grin and then played on and on without having to spend the other quarter, which he had blithely pocketed.

Months passed before Skip returned to the island with his family and a houseful of musicians. I was invited to stay and work with them in the bar and band business. I moved into a bedroom over the club and Lenox often stayed there, supplied with pizza and Pepsi, when I went downstairs to work. "Work" was drinking and dancing all night and then counting profits in the early morning—making it hard to distinguish from the after-work parties that ended with breakfast at the yacht club or the recording studio. At some point the next day, Lenox would always appear behind me, my grinning and tumbling shadow.

Not so often, I would follow Lenox onto the mountainside where he sometimes stayed with one of his aunties. This Auntie was a large, formidable woman who kept many children for many absent parents. She was an expert at emotional extortion. On each visit, she would tell me at length about the hardship that was her life and give me a long list of things that would help her endure. When I shopped for her, I added little gifts for her many children; Lenox reported to me that most of these candies and clothes were not distributed. More often, Lenox did Auntie's shopping for her, and he was clearly afraid of short-changing her. He told me he sometimes lost her quarters and was slapped across the face for this carelessness. I wondered how many times his face had to sting for him to become the secret pinball wizard.

Once, when I hadn't seen Lenox for a few days, I walked alone to Auntie's house to ask if my friend was all right. As I climbed unannounced up her path, I saw Lenox, naked and cowering, as Auntie flailed at him with something. When I interrupted, she explained that Lenox was supposed to take care of her goats but that he must have mistreated the nanny because her kid had been delivered dead. She had been thrashing Lenox with the stillborn fetus. Dumbfounded, I asked if I could take Lenox to town. Auntie gave me a list of things she wanted while Lenox got dressed. On our walk down the path Lenox just grinned up at me as though this was going to be another good day. There was some filmy stuff from the fetus still stuck to his dirty skin.

By this time I had grown to love Lenox in much the same way that I had long loved Paul McCartney. It was a wild, unrealistic love, a love that I had learned from the Romantic poets I had studied for so long. In short, I was in love with my idea of who Lenox might be.

I'D BEEN AWAY on Montserrat for seven months when my mother called, late one night, to tell me that my father had been killed in a small plane crash. I went in the dark to pick one of every kind of flower that grew in the jungle, and at dawn I went to the airport to stand by for the first available flight home. I waited a long time, and I will never again be able to smell those kinds of flowers without being sad. Late that night, I put my bouquet in the trash can and began my way through a succession of airports to be reunited with my family.

When my father's estate was settled, I learned that he had left me the financial resources to get started on any venture or adventure I might choose. The problem was, I hadn't a clue about what I wanted to do or who I wanted to be. My brother Barney suggested I work for a travel agency so that I might continue to wander aimlessly around the world while letting my mother believe I had a responsible job. That seemed reasonable.

I had been a travel consultant in Washington for about a year when my friend Susan McLeod called from Montserrat to tell me that Lenox was adrift, too. I had thought about Lenox often and had visited him once when my travel business had taken me close to his island. On that trip, Susan had helped me negotiate with Auntie to enroll Lenox at a private day school on Monserrat. I had given Auntie a small amount of my father's legacy to pay for Lenox's first semester and had left the island feeling fine about Lenox and myself. Now Susan was calling to say that both Lenox and the tuition had disappeared for a while, and only Lenox had reappeared. Susan reported that Lenox was now seen only at night, hanging around rum shops, begging for money. She said that he looked sad and afraid.

I announced to my family that I was going to use the rest of my inheritance to adopt a Montserratian street child. My mother knew, from years of study, the algebra of my emotions. In other words, she knew that if she displayed the perfectly reasonable reservations she might have about my announcement, her concerns would be met with stubborn resolve. So she offered me her support, and I began a lazy investigation into what this whimsy might entail. Then someone—maybe one of the adoption agents or immigration officers I casually interviewed—made the mistake of telling me that my scheme was impossible. From then on, I was no longer just daydreaming. I was determined.

An unmarried woman pursuing an interracial, international adoption was not commonplace in the early 1980s, and I worked hard to understand the intricate tangles of red tape. Only in retrospect did I realize that I had not expended anywhere near the same energy to look into my future and Lenox's and to try to understand the implications these actions would have for both of our lives. I only remember thinking that the word "mother" as others used it was not exactly what I had in mind.

Ludicrous as it may seem in retrospect, I never really thought parenthood through; adoption proceedings just seemed the most "Romantic" way to realize my plan. This plan was that Lenox and I should live a life in the States very much like the life we had led in the islands. I would continue to come and go as I pleased and Lenox, my young friend, could tag along when he wanted. I thought, quite simply, that I could easily share the privileges of my life and my society with this infamously independent child and that, consequently, both of our lives would be enriched. Key to this thought—and to the years of confusion that followed—are the words *simply* and *easily*.

I spent a year and a half traveling back and forth between Washington and Montserrat, taking care of logistics. On one trip I took Lenox a rough-terrain bicycle. When I returned a few months later, I met Lenox riding down the mountain on the island's sole paved road. He had one foot on the seat, the other on the handlebar, open hands flung wide in the air, his wide grin now filled with permanent teeth. His odometer showed he had ridden more than 1,000 miles. On another trip I took him his first pair of sneakers, and on another, a waterproof watch. I always took Auntie what she had requested from the trip before. I did not tell her the purpose of my trips until the paperwork was almost completed; then I invited her to the office of my Montserratian attorney to ask her about my plan. My lawyer explained to Auntie that it would be illegal to exchange money for the child, as she proposed; he did allow, however, that I could pay to install the telephone she wanted so that she might call Lenox in his new home. This seemed to make her very happy and she agreed that Lenox should go with "Miss Pat." That is what Lenox called me—until I put the plan to him. Then he said, "Sounds good to me, Mom!"

This is how I ended up in May 1985 in Monserrat's High Colonial Court, asking a panel of Her Majesty's lordships in white-powdered wigs for permission to adopt Lenox Barzey. After hearing careful evaluations from community representatives, the magistrates queried Lenox about his future. Lenox, standing tall in the short-pants suit I'd carried from K-Mart, said: "Your Lordships, I would like to go to America so that I can go to school so that I can study to be a judge." I was reminded, in that instant, of Lenox standing in front of the pinball machine asking, "How does it work?" Adoption granted. He told the flight attendant on the flight north that he was going to America so that he could go to school so that he could study to be a jet pilot. He flew the rest of the trip in the co-pilot's seat. As we circled Miami, Lenox announced to everyone over the PA system that "this America is sure one big island."

Lenox had accepted so many adventures with so much aplomb that I really didn't stop to think how strange everything must have seemed to him. As the airline captain escorted his new friend through the terminal to the immigration office, we walked toward an electric door that opened as we approached. Lenox stopped still, a puddle growing around his shoes, and began looking wildly about for jumbies, which is what the islanders call evil spirits. The captain and I stepped onto and off of the rubber carpet as the door opened and shut, and soon Lenox was laughing with us. He collected his "green card" and everyone's best wishes, and we continued to Washington. Lenox told the taxi driver who drove us from National Airport that he wanted to be a chauffeur one day, and when we arrived at my mother's house the driver refused to take our fare for his service.

As soon as we were inside, Lenox, like most weary travelers, asked for directions to the bathroom. I waited a long time for him to return so that I could introduce him to the rest of his family. When I finally went looking for him, I found him frantically stepping on and off the small oriental rug that my mother had placed in front of the bathroom door. When I turned the handle and pushed the door open, he just grinned up at me and rushed in.

Lenox was almost ten years old when he arrived in the United States and was enrolled, with no documented personal history, in the fourth grade of a Montgomery County public school. As his interest shifted from flush toilets to video games, he became the subject of myriad medical and educational tests. I remember most vividly the intelligence tests that were administered a few days before his first Christmas here. It was explained to me over that holiday that Lenox's test results defined him as mildly retarded. When asked to name the four seasons of the year, Lenox (who had immigrated on June 14, Flag Day, and thought that all the flags in Washington flew for his welcome) recited, "Halloween, Thanksgiving, Christmas and New Year's." When shown a drawing of a chest of drawers and asked, "What's wrong with this picture?" he replied that nothing was wrong. For six months Lenox had had a dresser at our house with handles missing, much like the one in the picture. The test administrators agreed that "cultural difference" should be factored into the analysis of Lenox's test results. I knew, but did not explain, that the culture from which Lenox came—an English-speaking, educated society—was not radically different from American culture. Lenox's disadvantages had been familial, not cultural. But I accepted this rationale and the alternative testing methods that it allowed.

After another battery of tests, which emphasized verbal skills, I was told that Lenox was "gifted." The school system carefully ignored these conflicting diagnoses, and Lenox's course of instruction presumed that he was neither retarded nor gifted.

I began to suspect that he was both.

Superficially, Lenox acclimated well. The same grace with which he seduced tourists on Montserrat worked as well on teachers and counselors in Chevy Chase. His looks, agility and social daring made him a kingpin among neighborhood children. The public who knew of our history thought that Lenox was very lucky and that I was very courageous.

In private, we were both confused and afraid.

Soon after we arrived in the States, I discovered that Lenox kept caches of food and loose change hidden in his room. I assumed this to be an understandable reaction to past insecurities, so I made every effort to assure Lenox that we would always be together. Then I would put him to bed, leaving him alone or with my mother. My naive plan was working: My good friend Lenox was safe in my world and I was still out on the town.

I refer to this, in retrospect, as my period of "Montessori motherhood." Lenox was allowed to do what he wanted in exchange for my being able to do what I wanted. The problem with this plan was that our wishes were often in conflict. What Lenox wanted the most was my undivided attention. What I wanted most, more and more often, was the unfettered life I had traded away. This "infamously independent" child became, in one psychologist's term, "intrusively possessive." He had temper tantrums when I made plans that did not include him, and he abused the men I went out with. He greeted one of my dates at the door with a raised ball-peen hammer. When asked, by this good-natured caller, if he wanted to join us for dinner, he said no. He argued that if people saw us out with a white man they would draw the conclusion that Lenox, and not my date, was the outsider. "People might think you found me on the street or something," he said defiantly.

As the months passed, I became even more confused and afraid than Lenox. He was not the person I had imagined him to be, and I feared my love for him was not great enough to guide either one of us through the confusion of who he really was. I had desperate dreams in which

I returned Lenox to Montserrat. Friends on the island reported that Auntie used the phone I had installed to call Radio Antilles and ask the broadcasters to relay her "best wishes to the queen." But she never called to ask for or about Lenox. I had, after all, told her that Lenox would have a fine life as my son. I was no longer sure of this.

I *was* sure, after extensive searching, that adoption, unlike many legal contracts, has no escape clause.

When Lenox was eleven, we moved from Chevy Chase back to Chestertown. My friends Meredith Davies and David Wheelan, administrators at Washington College, had arranged for a job interview for me at my *alma mater*. I hoped that the small careful town would share in my overwhelming parenting responsibilities. I knew by now that I could not manage these by myself.

Upon entering Chestertown Middle School, Lenox began to evidence behavior and learning problems. Lenox's most confounding disability was described as an inability to conceptualize or to deal with abstractions. He could read a seventh-grade book, albeit slowly, and recall the clothing the characters had worn and the words they had said. But when asked, "What was the main idea of the story?" he could not respond. His teachers suggested that I help him understand classroom concepts by trying to make them more concrete. This was easy enough when Lenox was figuring math problems about quarters and nickels and dimes. It was not so easy when Kafka appeared on his summer reading list. Facetiously, I asked his teacher where Lenox and I might purchase Greyhound tickets to Hell. What I knew, but could not admit, was that we were already there.

My stubborn scheme—that Lenox and I would evade change—was working. It was making both of us more miserable than ever. Though I worked long hours as Washington College's alumni director and Lenox struggled through school, we both spent our unscheduled time clinging to previous lifestyles. I still hung out at the local nightclub, and Lenox traveled the streets on his bicycle. He soon had many friends—classmates and college students. He rarely spoke of them; instead he talked endlessly about bicycles and watches. I remember wondering if these, the things I had carried to him on Montserrat, were not only material obsessions but somehow symbols of our earlier relationship that had, by now, gone so wrong. But I was otherwise uninterested—uninterested, that is, until one gruesome evening when, in the course of collecting laundry, I found a drawer full of watches in Lenox's room. Confronted, he would not tell me how he had acquired them. The next day I queried clerks at local stores. Lenox hung around, they said, but no thefts had been reported. Matt Zeuch, a college student who had befriended Lenox, hesitantly told me of missing some cash and expensive sunglasses, but he insisted on giving Lenox the benefit of the doubt. Lenox was dumb when I asked him again, and he was dumb when I put forth my next plan.

This plan was "Mussolini Motherhood." Lenox had never removed the waterproof watch I had given him on Montserrat years earlier. When I took this from his wrist it felt—to both of us, I think now—that I was breaking a tangible bond. I told him that he could not wear a watch again until he had earned my trust. In the meantime, I would be his timekeeper, and his day would be rigorously scheduled. Betsy and Tom Herr, careful friends of mine, gave Lenox an after-school job at Anthony's, their florist and landscaping business, so that, together, we could account for all of his time. As months passed, it seemed that Tom and Lenox were becoming confidants, but Lenox's confidence was of a different sort: Tom told me that he wept when he caught Lenox stealing from his cash register, but that Lenox remained dry-eyed. He seemed disturbingly undisturbed that Tom was terminating his job and their friendship.

Not long after that, Lenox and I were side by side in the kitchen at suppertime when his pocket emitted six beeps. He froze. I took a hammer from the tool drawer and marched him through the back door. I took the watch from his pocket and laid it on the cement stoop. I handed him the hammer and told him to smash the watch. He trembled and could not. I took the hammer from him and with one whack, powered with all my despair, smashed its face to smithereens. When I looked up, I saw that Lenox's once-bright eyes were empty.

The pinball machine also came back to haunt us. One Sunday morning, the police came to our door to question Lenox. Their story had a gang of boys visiting video machines in town, opening the coin deposit with a screwdriver, playing games with the booty until bored, and then moving on to the next machine. The other boys had, upon questioning, returned their share of stolen quarters and offered up Lenox as their leader. The machines gave supporting evidence: The high-scorer, this time, was Lenox Barzey *Trams*. Our good police advised that Lenox turn himself in to the store managers and make restitution. Having completed these shameful introductions, I asked Lenox if his raiders had hit any other machines that the police did not know about. Lenox said they had not.

On Monday morning when I reported to work at the college, Jerry Roderick, the chief of security, was waiting in my office with a report that all the video machines in our Student Center had been vandalized and that Lenox was a suspect. He heard, in my sobs, that Lenox and I were both in desperate need of help. He made a call to a friend of his who was a warden at the local detention center. Yet another plan was devised: I called the principal of Lenox's school and told her that my friend in uniform would be coming to take Lenox out of class for another kind of lesson. Then I drove to the jail, where the warden gently advised me that I must not interfere in what I was about to see. Then, as Lenox was led through the door by college security, the warden and another officer rushed out to meet them. I watched through a window as the warden pushed my now thirteen-year-old son so that his face and shoulders were pressed against the wall while the other officer cuffed his wrists. I was trembling so that I could barely stand. Lenox went limp as the officers led him out of my sight. Back in his office, the warden explained that Lenox was being fingerprinted and photographed, as if this were a real arrest. Then he would spend some time in a cell with a trustee—a rehabilitated prisoner trusted to scare sense into adolescents. Hours passed before Lenox returned. As I drove Lenox home from the detention center, I could not read any fear in his face. His blank stare filled me, on the other hand, with an unshakable sense of terror.

I made an appointment with a psychiatrist who looked so much like Sigmund Freud that it would have been funny under any other circumstances. After long interviews with me about Lenox's past, and long interviews with Lenox, he told me that Lenox was a sociopath. I had read enough murder mysteries to understand the implications of this. "Dr. Freud" offered his explanation. He said that one's sense of ego was defined early in life and determined by one's relationship to one's family. Children from dysfunctional homes, he continued, often have an especially strong sense of self, good or bad, as this ego is their only defense against an emotionally or physically destructive family. He hypothesized that Lenox, who had grown up without family or guidance, was not egocentric but egoless. He said that my friend's obvious charm was not sophistication but survival instinct. Lenox, according to "Freud," was incapable of being sensitive to others' feelings because, as a defense against his early circumstances, he had not allowed himself to have feelings. He wasn't disregarding the distinction between good and bad or right and wrong; he had never learned to make these distinctions. Talking to Lenox about love and trust, he explained, was like telling a blind person about blues and greens. The psychiatrist's prognosis was pessimistic. It was "too late," he believed, to change the thirteen-year course of Lenox's life. He refused to offer me the hope I wanted. And in refusing this, he presented Lenox and me with the challenge that would change our lives. I had one plan left. It would be unusually unoriginal, and it would be neither simple nor easy.

My last desperate plan was "motherhood."

Slowly, in this gloomy doctor's office a light had gone on in my head. Lenox's inability to conceptualize was not just a reading disability—it was a living disability. Lenox's teachers had been working to help him understand the definitions of words and how they fit together. I had been trying to explain my definitions of family and society and how we all fit together. The integral piece of this puzzle, the one we had overlooked or taken for granted, was Lenox's definition of himself. He had none. Because "sociopath" was an unacceptable conclusion for me, I chose instead to think of this apparently savvy teenager as an emotional infant. And with this insight, we began again. This time, at the beginning.

First, my life had to be restructured to suit a young son instead of a visiting friend. Though our family had been subjected to whimsical plans, our household had never had a real routine. Lenox's independence had permitted my own, and this had been selfishly important to me. It did not occur to me that my resolute independence and my feelings of loneliness were in any way interdependent. I just figured I had nothing left to lose. So Lenox and I began to keep a schedule of each other's company that was no more flexible than the feeding schedule for an infant. And the most remarkable effect of this was the relief that I felt. When I sacrificed my frantic nights on the town for quiet family evenings and early bedtimes, I was genuinely surprised to feel less tired and strangely content. Nor had I supposed that Lenox's mood changes had been, or would be, so dependent on mine.

When, in the previous three years, I had looked at Lenox as my independent companion, I was always disappointed that he did not live up to my expectations. When I looked at him now as my dependent charge, I was delighted when he, often, exceeded my expectations. I no longer assumed that Lenox understood the difference between good and bad feelings or right and wrong actions. So Lenox and I began to talk together in simple language about simple things that were considered right and wrong and that made us feel, consequently, good or bad. We spent time together trying to explain our feelings about ourselves, and one another. At first, Lenox was not very good at this exercise. When I asked him how he felt about some incident in our day he would just shrug. This, I now reasoned, was not apathy but a real inability to understand and, hence, express what was happening in his heart.

So I tried to tell Lenox about every little thing I noticed he was doing right and how good this made me feel. In the evening, Lenox wanted to hear me tell the story of our day. In this recitation, I tried to include each of the kind gestures and good judgments Lenox had made since that morning. The stories grew longer and longer. This, I could tell, was giving Lenox a definition of himself that he was beginning to trust and be proud of. Then Lenox, eager to participate, began to reciprocate with his stories about our day and all the things I had done that made him feel good.

I remember thinking, "So this is how it works."

One night Lenox told me that a policeman had come into his classroom that day. He said he wasn't afraid because he hadn't done anything wrong. I realized then that Lenox must have been very afraid on the day of his mock-arrest even though he had never said so. He laughed when he told me that the officer had come, in uniform, to excuse his daughter for a dentist appointment. Lenox said, "I felt good, Mom."

Another night, much later, an acquaintance/crush of mine named Eric Dennard stopped by while Lenox and I were fixing supper. He had hoped, he said, to take me out for dinner. I looked anxiously at Lenox, who said, "I'll be okay by myself. Go out and have fun, Mom." I knew, in that very instant, that Lenox and I were going to make it together.

On Christmas Day, in that crisis-less year, Tom Herr came to visit. He brought a poinsettia for me and a deal for Lenox. Though he would not excuse Lenox for betraying his trust, he had decided to offer his forgiveness—and a job in his greenhouse—as a holiday bargain. On Christmas night, Lenox told me that the most precious gift he had received that day was that of a second chance.

From then on Lenox went to work every day after school and came home tired but happy. His weekly checks, as agreed, were made payable to me. I kept this pay in an account, which Lenox was allowed to spend with supervision. He had collected almost $100 before he made his first withdrawal, along with a request. He had written a letter addressed to his "big brother" Matt Zeuch. Would I trust him enough to put $50 of his money in the envelope without reading the letter? I told him that I trusted him, and that he could trust me. He went to school and I read the letter. It was a sad and wonderful confession that he had once stolen a pair of sunglasses from this close friend. The letter was a promise to continue payments until the sunglasses could be replaced. I sent the money with the letter and kept my mouth shut. Lenox chose to read me the quick response. Matt wrote that he happened to find Ray-Bans on sale that very day and was returning to Lenox the $10 change from the purchase with his love and respect.

That summer, my mother—Lenox's grandmother—treated him to a week of overnight camp. On this trip to the Chesapeake Bay, Lenox said to me, "I had a dream last night, Mom. I dreamed that one day my children will be judged not by the color of their skin but by the content of their char.... No wait...! That was somebody else's dream. I dreamed that there was a fat kid on the bunk above and the bed collapsed and crushed me." This twisted humor from my passenger caught me off guard. and I had a giggle attack on the highway. Lenox laughed with me. It was the first time in four years that this sound from him seemed unaffected. I remember being overwhelmed with the joy of the moment. And in my memory, that is when the light came back into his eyes.

The next year we visited a Quaker boarding school where my sister Penny had been a student. This trip included a casual visit to the admissions office that turned into a weekend on the campus for Lenox. Before long he had been accepted into the school's ninth grade. He received his invitation with mixed feelings: he felt proud to be awarded the privilege of a place in the community, but he was afraid as well. What, he wondered, would a black kid with a white mother say to new friends when they asked him about his history? The next weekend we posed a "family" photograph with Lenox's grandmother, Tom Herr, Matt Zeuch, Eric Dennard, et al., in or under the branches of the big maple in our front yard. Now, we explained, Lenox had a "family tree" to show his classmates. He was still afraid. How, he wondered, could he tell the truth about his life without informing people that he had been a thief? And if he told the truth, wouldn't he always be a suspect if crimes were committed at his new school?

A few days after Lenox started at the Sandy Spring Friends School, I was pulled from a meeting to answer a call from one of his teachers. I reacted with reflexive dread. This teacher told me there had been a theft in Lenox's dorm. All the students had been called together. Lenox, she said, knew that he was not a suspect, but he chose to stand on this occasion to tell his life's story. Later, when everyone was in study hall, the stolen items had been mysteriously replaced. She apologized for interrupting my day, but she thought I should know about this.

Lenox turned sixteen that semester. I planned that Lenox's dorm head should present him with my present at breakfast on his birthday. When she called me that morning, she reported that Lenox had knocked on her door at one minute past midnight and asked to receive his package. She said he seemed very pleased—but not very surprised—to find a watch inside.

In our end-of-the-year conference, the consensus was that Lenox's social triumphs outweighed his academic frustrations, and the school volunteered special courses in exchange for the example of his spirit.

While Lenox was away for the tenth grade, our friend Eric was found to have a terminal illness. I spent most of that winter on the road, traveling between Eric's isolated art studio in Dorchester County where he needed to work, Johns Hopkins Hospital in Baltimore, and my house on the Chester River where he received the attention of his many friends. By the time Lenox arrived home for summer vacation, the logistics of cancer were beginning to exhaust my spirit and the patience of my employer. Without calling any attention to his actions, Lenox inserted himself in our routine. With Tom's support, he scheduled his summer job hours around daily commutes to chemotherapy. Eric appreciated this friendly escort. Lenox, he said, had an uncanny ability for drawing attention to himself and away from everyone's sickness. When I had to be absent in the evening, Lenox made casual excuses to stay home. Once Eric reported to me that Lenox had pulled a chair into the hall by his door and sat there quietly alert while he thought his friend was sleeping. In spite of his devastating disease, Eric was intent on sharing delight. He reminded us every day that life was a wonderful adventure. Eric, I knew, was trying to teach Lenox about the joy of everyday things. Lenox, I knew, was learning about extraordinary courage. Lenox no longer needed coaching about responsibilities. He assumed his, and many of mine, without being asked. Once, after Lenox had relieved me of a long day in an outpatient clinic, allowing me a long day in the office, I said: "For all the trouble we went through in becoming a family, you're paying me back in spades." Lenox, having never heard this expression before, replied, "You're welcome in honkeys."

It was Lenox's decision to stay at home for eleventh grade. Three weeks after he returned to public school, he announced that he had been elected president of the Student Government Association at Kent County High School. I said, "You mean you've been elected the president of a club represented on the SGA." He said, "No, Mom, I'm the president of the SGA." I said, "You mean you're the president of your junior class?" He said matter-of-factly, "No, Mom, I'm the head Negro in charge, and I need *Somebody's Book of Preliminary Procedure*." This election report was reconfirmed weeks later when Lenox was invited to a Baltimore television station to be introduced, as president of his school, to the studio audience. Lenox wrote on the invitation envelope, "It's Acedemic." When a friend saw this he told Lenox, "It's better to look good than to spell good. Just put a slide rule in your shirt pocket for the occasion." Lenox said, "A what?"

Lenox made the honor roll at Kent County High School. Eric was very sick and in always-present pain when Lenox told him this. Our friend struggled to surface through morphine to tell Lenox how very proud he was. The next day at the hospital, Eric announced to everyone that Lenox had made the National Honor Society. I told Lenox that, if Eric had lived to keep telling this story, Lenox eventually would have been nominated for a Nobel Prize in algebra. Eric did not live long enough. He died a few days later in his own bed. I was holding him and his closest friends were all near. First, we reported Eric's death to his many doctors, who were saddened by the news. Next, I asked my best friend Davies to find my son at school and ask him to call me. When I told Lenox that Eric had died bravely and peacefully, he said, "That's good." My son's response, in contrast to others' sympathy, stunned me at first. And then I realized that Lenox, in his unrehearsed response, had remembered Eric's pain before he felt his own. The pain did set in, but Lenox bore it with courage. He told me that Eric had once said, "Nobody's allowed to cry unless I do." Lenox never saw Eric cry. He only remembers his laugh.

Eric might have laughed upon overhearing a phone call made to Lenox a few months later. I could tell from Lenox's tone of voice that the person on the other end of the phone was not, per usual, making a date to cruise for girls in the shopping center parking lot. I heard Lenox say, "I am honored by the invitation, but you have to understand I have a lacrosse game that day." I motioned for his attention, he read my lips and replied, "I am invited to meet with President Clinton." I

PHOTO: DMITRI FOTOS

Pat and Lenox Trams grew up together —with the help of friends and neighbors in Chestertown—and were a perfectly functional family by the time this portrait was taken in 1995.

said I would write a letter of excuse to his lacrosse coach in exchange for an explanation. And this is how I learned that MTV producers had been around the country asking high school students to share ideas with the president. Lenox re-created his audition for me, reporting that he had said: "Teenagers who hurt other people are put on TV news, but teenagers who help other people are not. The president should know that the crime rate would probably drop if good citizens got to be on TV as much as criminals." I could hear ghostly pinballs racking up points. Adoption granted. Audition over. And so, the president of the Kent County High School Student Government Association went off to meet the President of the United States in an MTV forum about teenagers and crime. In light of our past experiences, this invitation might seem to carry with it great irony. The expression "funny fate" passed through my mind, until I realized that Lenox, not fate, had changed our lives. Despite "Dr. Freud's" diagnosis, Lenox had been determined to grow, and he had decided to bring me along with him.

I remember Lenox calling me from boarding school three years ago to tell me that he had fallen in love "for the first and last time." Soon after, I was introduced to the focus of Lenox's school year, and the recipient of a summer of long-distance calls. I never doubted that this was true love. Lenox would often pause in mid-mundanity to ask me, "Isn't life great!" But then, in the course of forever, Lenox had moved on to Kent County High, and I was soon introduced to another special girl. I remember asking Lenox, in all affected seriousness, "But what about 'forever'?" Lenox turned to me with genuine seriousness and sad concern. "Mom," he said, "you have a lot to learn about love."

And I thought I had learned so much.

Editor's Note: P. Trams Hollingsworth, a gardener, lives with her husband, Bill, in Chestertown. Lenox Trams is now a detective for the Town of Easton Police. The orphan from Montserrat married Diana, a beauty from Maine, in the summer of 2002. They welcomed their first child, a son named Tyler, on July 11, 2005.

George Washington in Kent County
Or, the Curse of the Rock Hall Ferry

JOHN R. BOHRER

HOW MANY YEARS does it take to certify a great American curse? Must it be borne out of incompetence? Is the involvement of a famous figure necessary?

The Boston Red Sox would affirm all three questions thus: eighty-nine years, a brainless trade with the Yankees and Babe Ruth. If these are the true qualities of a curse, Kent County does even better. Try 142 years, inept sailing in a dark storm and President George Washington.

This curse kept sitting presidents out of the county from 1791 to 1933. In that time, thirty American Presidents passed through the Oval Office—scarcely fifty miles away as the crow flies—without once passing through Kent County. A period so long devoid of any notable travelers, people began forgetting they had *ever* passed by. An 1871 article in *Harper's Magazine* claimed the Eastern Shore was "a ground never trodden by the tourist."

But this was not true and in 1932, Kent County decided to do something about it. Like the Sox's 2004 "Keep the Faith" billboards around Back Bay, the citizens of Chestertown erected a historical marker in the center of town. The sign (still standing today) boasts of the county's rich colonial history and commemorates the visits of the first president:

"George Washington made eight known visits here between 1756 and 1793."

Although—as we shall see—that marker may have broken the curse, careful research reveals that the information is not wholly accurate. But it is true that Washington had a nearly lifelong acquaintance with this area. Chestertown knew him from his twenties into his sixties, from his days as a militiaman to his tenure as commander-in-chief.

The reason for all these visits is that in the 18th century, Kent County lay on one of the two main north-south travel routes through the Chesapeake region. One route, on the Western Shore, ran through Anne Arundel County, bypassing Annapolis, and then continued through Baltimore and around the top of the Bay. On the other route, travelers would board a ferryboat in Annapolis and cross the Bay to Rock Hall, proceed to Chestertown (where they often stopped for food, drink and lodging), and then continue through Georgetown and into Cecil County. The two routes converged near New Castle, Delaware, and continued on toward Philadelphia (then the leading city in the American colonies) and further north.

Tracing Washington's trips to Chestertown therefore means tracing his quest—and, of course, attainment—of prominence beyond his native province of Virginia. From his secluded country seat on the Potomac, he would repeatedly set out northwards in search of glory.

FIRST VISIT: FEBRUARY 1756 (POSSIBLE)

It is widely believed that George Washington's military career began during the French and Indian War. But in fact, it started two years before that war was officially declared. In the summer of 1754, Governor Robert Dinwiddie sent Washington, as lieutenant-colonel of militia, into the Ohio Country to remove the French by force. Young Washington's troops were attacked and defeated at Fort Necessity. Though off to a bad start, he was still optimistic about a military career; a year later, he accepted the command of the Virginia Regiment. And higher honors than these colonial appointments still beckoned: James MacGregor Burns and Susan

Dunn describe this period as Washington's "quest for a holy grail" in the form of a royal commission in the British army.

It is possible this quest brought Washington to Kent County for the first time. It was the winter of 1756, and young Colonel Washington, hoping to advance his career, was on his way to Boston to meet with Governor William Shirley of Massachusetts. His diary places him in Bladensburg, Maryland, on February 4, and in Philadelphia on February 8. Some historians have speculated that those three lost days were spent in Annapolis and on the Eastern Shore, since after a later trip through Kent County, Washington stopped in Annapolis and then stayed in Bladensburg.

Regardless of how he got there, in Boston, Washington met with Governor Shirley, the senior officer of British forces in America, to take care of some military business and seek commissions for himself and his men in the British army. In numerous letters preceding the meeting, Washington asked for better supplies for his troops, with an emphasis on clothing. A royal commission could solve the problem. Although Governor Shirley found him impressive enough to grant him rank over a British captain, the main purpose of the visit failed: he did not give Washington or his men commissions in the British army.

SECOND VISIT: MARCH 1756 (POSSIBLE)

It is also possible that Washington passed through Kent County on his return from Boston the following month. This time, his diary places him in Chester, Pennsylvania, on March 21, and back in Alexandria by March 23, while an Annapolis newspaper records that he "came to town from the Northward" on March 22, spending the night before setting off for Virginia the next morning. If Washington had boasted of his upcoming meeting with Shirley during his trip northward in February, it is likely he had no desire to share the embarrassing results during his return in March. With nothing to celebrate, the young man could have traveled quickly through the Eastern Shore and Annapolis, and made the trip in two days.

THIRD VISIT: FEBRUARY 1757

But there is a more certain early instance in which Washington passed through Kent County. A year after the Boston journey, Washington traveled to Philadelphia to meet with Virginia governor Lord Loudon and the governors of the other southern colonies. According to his diary, on February 15 Washington was in Annapolis and mentioned ferrying across the Potomac. He wrote, "Ditto at N. Town," on the nineteenth, indicating he had ferried to Kent County: "New Town" or "Newtown on Chester" was then the common name for Chestertown. His expense account for the trip also indicates that he spent ten shillings while in town, which probably indicates that he spent the night in a tavern here. Washington would reach Philadelphia perhaps two days later, three at the latest.

At Philadelphia, Washington delivered a memorial to John Campbell, Earl of Loudon, on the trials of the Virginia Regiment, pleading on behalf of his men for a commission. "Whereas, the disregarding the faithful Services, of any Body of His Majesty's Subjects," he began, "tends to discourage Merit, and lessen that generous Emulation, Spirit, and laudable Ambition so necessary to prevail in an Army...." Again, however, Washington bolstered his reputation but failed to secure his commission.

FOURTH VISIT: MARCH 1757 (POSSIBLE)

Washington's second 1757 passage through Kent County is less well-documented than his first. The southern governors' conference ended on March 23, and Washington was present in Annapolis on the thirtieth. It is more than likely that he was in Kent County sometime between the twenty-sixth and twenty-ninth.

FIFTH VISIT: MAY 1773

It would be more than fifteen years before Washington passed through Chestertown again. That decade and a half had seen great changes in his life. In 1758, he had captured Fort Duquesne in a less-than-heroic fashion (the French retreated before his men could fire even a single shot) but, a year later, he left the military, deciding that landholding and politics were better outlets for his ambitions. He had married a wealthy widow, Martha Dandridge Custis, and won a seat in the Virginia House of Burgesses in 1759. He had collected some 2,000 acres through his military service and in 1771, inherited his prized Mount Vernon. After a lackluster start in politics, Washington finally took up against British policies in the spring of 1769, at the urging of more vocal colleagues such as Patrick Henry.

Washington's fifth visit to Chestertown—one of the best-documented—was occasioned by the departure of his stepson, John "Jacky" Parke Custis, to be enrolled at King's College in New York (now Columbia University). Washington had made Custis's selection for him after having deliberated over the choice of colleges in letters with the Rev. John Boucher. In one dated January 7, 1773, Washington writes, "I cannot think William & Mary College a desirable place to send Jack Custis to—the Inattention of the Masters, added to the number of Hollidays, is the subject of general complaint; & affords no pleasing prospect to a youth who has a good deal to attain." Washington also considered European institutions, suggested earlier by Boucher, out of the question, writing "there no longer seems to be any thoughts of him crossing the Atlantick." He concluded that he had "determined to send him to the Philadelphia College" (now the University of Pennsylvania), noting that "being nearer, [it] is more agreeable to his Mother." Washington made mention of his "small acquaintance" with the college's president, William Smith, and said that he would "be very glad to consult Dr. Smith on the terms it is proper for him to enter College," but asked Boucher to write a letter of recommendation for Jacky as well.

Boucher, however, sent a long letter back to Washington two weeks later, agreeing to help but not endorsing his decision. Boucher claimed "the highest Respect" for Dr. Smith's character, but added that he had "no personal acquaintance"; however, he did have a close relationship with Dr. Myles Cooper of King's College, as an honorary alumnus of the school. While he described other American institutions as closer to "Scotld, Leyden, Gottingen, Geneva," he claimed that King's College and William & Mary resembled "Oxford & Cambridge." This must have whetted the appetite of rank-conscious Washington. Boucher also argued that New York, "the most fashionable & polite Place on the Continent," would be a better learning environment for young Custis. Boucher effectively persuaded Washington and, a few months later, the 16-year-old Jacky—accompanied by his stepfather—was on his way north.

Washington stayed in Chestertown four days into his journey, on May 13. He had left Mount Vernon on May 10 and met Jacky at Mount Airy, the home of Benedict Calvert in Prince George's County, Maryland. (Jacky had arrived there two days earlier to visit with his fiancée, Nelly, who was Calvert's daughter.) On the second and third nights of his journey, Washington stayed in Annapolis with Governor Robert Eden, who then accompanied the men to Philadelphia to watch his horse race at the Jockey Club.

Washington, Custis and Eden took a two-and-a-half-hour ferry ride across the Chesapeake Bay from Annapolis to Rock Hall and then rode to what Washington now called in his diary "Chester Town." (The old name of "New Town" was by then used less frequently.)

Chestertown at this time was a thriving port of entry for the upper Eastern Shore, and many merchants could be found near the water. One such merchant was the governor's brother, Captain Thomas Eden, whose ship, the *Annapolis*, was there. That afternoon, Washington dined aboard Captain Eden's boat on the Chester River.

His next diary entry for that day, "Supped & lodgd at Mr Ringolds," has caused much local speculation. There were three different Ringgold households along Water Street, but the one where the men spent the evening was probably that of Thomas Ringgold V and his wife, Mary Galloway Ringgold—and what is now known as the Hynson-Ringgold House. Ringgold's father, who had died the year before, was a business acquaintance of both Washington and Eden, and he had stayed overnight at Mount Vernon in 1771 (accompanied by Samuel Galloway, who was Mary's father and the elder Ringgold's business partner in slave-trading and other pursuits).

Washington, Custis and Eden left Chestertown the next day, continuing their leisurely trip only as far as Georgetown, a mere sixteen miles away. After a night visiting Daniel Charles Heath, (nephew of Daniel Dulany, Jr., a prominent Maryland lawyer and friend of Governor Eden), they continued on into Delaware and Pennsylvania. Washington would take the Western Shore route on his return to Virginia.

SIXTH VISIT: SEPTEMBER 1774

Not long after Washington returned home, anger surged up and down the entire coast in response to Parliament's passage of the Tea Act. At the Boston Tea Party, angry colonists protested by dressing as Indians and dumping tea into the Boston Harbor. The Coercive Acts of the following spring, closing the port of Boston and imposing other hardships against the people of Massachusetts, sent further shock waves through the colonies, especially in ports like Chestertown. Virginia's governor, Lord Dunmore, feared similar retribution and, when the House of Burgesses expressed its outrage at Parliament, he dissolved the body. The Burgesses unofficially assembled at the Raleigh Tavern in Williamsburg and called for an annual Continental Congress. And Washington devoted himself to the colonial struggle. In early August of 1774, he was elected by the first Virginia Convention to attend the First Continental Congress in Philadelphia.

This call to service drew Washington back to Kent County. He invited Richard Henry Lee to come with him if he were to go "by Land, instead of water," but ultimately traveled with Patrick Henry and Edmund Pendleton. Henry and Pendleton arrived at Mount Vernon on August 30 and left on August 31. (According to Pendleton, Mrs. Washington urged them on their departure to "stand firm in their demands against the British ministry.")

On this trip, Washington would not take his time. The party reached Rock Hall the next evening. They had stopped at Queen Anne in Prince George's County and dined in Annapolis. The men ferried over to Rock Hall, by which time it was too late to trek to Chestertown, so they stayed at a ferry-house run by James Hodges, as indicated by Washington's expense ledger. The group spent most of the day in Rock Hall, according to Washington's diary, "waiting for [his] Horses," which may have been with his body servant, William Lee. They spent that night, September 2, in Chestertown. They must have been making up for lost time, because in the morning, they did not wait to have breakfast in Chestertown. The men went north to Down's Cross Roads, which is now called Galena. Perhaps they feared a storm, for it was "Cloudy & Cool" by Washington's account, and had rained the previous night. They ate breakfast at Down's tavern, run by William Down, and reached Delaware by mid-morning.

This trip to Philadelphia would certainly be more successful than the last for Washington, because this time he would not feel excluded from the action. He learned much from the other delegates at the Congress. During his time in the city, one of the many intelligent and affluent Americans he dined with was James Tilghman, Sr., a part-time resident of Kent County and the father of Tench Tilghman, who would serve as Washington's aide throughout the coming war. Washington also left a positive impression on many fellow delegates whom he was meeting for the first time, especially John Adams of the Massachusetts delegation.

SEVENTH VISIT: OCTOBER 1774

At the conclusion of the First Continental Congress on October 26, 1774, Washington was one of two remaining Virginia delegates, but he wasted no time on his way home. He retraced his path down the Shore in remarkable time, reaching Newcastle on the first night of his trip and "New town upon Chester" by the second night. (He had stopped at Down's Crossroads to dine along the way.) On the morning of October 29, Washington breakfasted in Rock Hall and arrived at Annapolis sometime in the afternoon. He would be home by three pm the next day.

* * *

IT WOULD BE NEARLY A DECADE before Washington passed through Kent County again. Although the Chestertown historical marker claims the route to be "the most traveled highway situated between north and south in the Revolutionary Period," Washington did not pass through once during the war itself.

Kent County experienced changes during the Revolutionary War period that mark it still today. In 1780, the county seat made the official name change to Chestertown. The town also received the academic who had had a "small acquaintance" with Washington many years earlier. In 1779, William Smith found himself deposed as provost of the College of Philadelphia in a takeover by the state legislature and the college's new trustees. On February 27, 1780, he took up the position of rector of Chester parish in Kent County, now Emmanuel Episcopal Church. Smith, ever the academic he had been in Philadelphia, took an interest in the Kent County Free School.

On July 8, 1782, Dr. Smith wrote to General Washington at his military headquarters in Newburgh, New York, informing him that the Maryland Legislature had renamed the Kent County School, "Washington College." Washington had likely heard of and seen the school, due to his trips to Chestertown and having sat for Charles Willson Peale, whose father had once served as headmaster.

Washington received the letter from Colonel Tench Tilghman on August 8, and wrote back ten days later, endorsing the honor. On August 18, he wrote to Smith promising a "Fifty Guineas" donation: a "trifling sum," he apologized, but "an earnest of my wishes for the prosperity of this Seminary." To the college, the generosity of such a famous donor would prove anything but trifling, but Washington apparently found many things to be "trifles" in the 1780s, as the word appears in numerous letters. Defeating the most powerful nation in the world must put many things on a different scale.

Washington continued in his letter: "With much pleasure should I consent to have my name enrolled among the worthy Visitors and Governors of this College, but convinced as I am, that it never will be in my power to give the attendance wch. by Law is required, my name could only be inserted to the exclusion of some other, whose abilities and proximity might enable him to become a more useful member." Smith, however—never one to take no for an answer—had no such qualms about Washington's busy schedule, and he was duly appointed to the college's board.

Washington must truly have found the donation "trifling," for he forgot about it, failing to mention fifty guineas to his wartime accountant and comptroller of Congress, James Milligan. In December of 1782, Smith called upon Robert Morris in Philadelphia to collect Washington's fifty guineas, to buy "an Elegant Air-Pump & some optical Instruments." Morris forwarded the sum to Smith later that month, and then deducted the money from Washington's account.

It was not until over a year later, when revising Washington's expenditures since the outset of the war, that Milligan discovered and questioned Washington about the mysterious donation to a "Washington College in Maryland." Washington then acknowledged the expense in a letter of February 18, 1784 to Milligan, as being "perfectly just, & ought not to have been omitted by me, for I well recollect it was the desire of Mr Morris, that this sum might be carried to the credit of my public accots, & I certainly meant to do it, altho' it has been omitted." A trifling sum, indeed.

EIGHTH VISIT: APRIL 1784

Washington's concerns at the time had more to do with the young country than the young college. Like Rome's Cincinnatus, Washington had defeated the enemy and then relinquished his command. His resignation came with regrets. With the British defeated, Washington strongly believed that the country needed a common goal. Congressional power was dwindling. The states needed a "Supreme Power to regulate and govern the general concerns." Washington again had to leave his Mount Vernon courtyard to tend his national garden.

On New Year's Day, 1784, Washington called the State Societies of the Cincinnati, leading officers of the Revolutionary War, to a national meeting. As the organization's president, Washington determined to meet at the Old City Tavern on the first Monday of May.

Washington set out for Philadelphia on April 26, 1784. In his list of expenditures for the trip, Washington paid for "Ferriages to Rock-hall pr. Middleton," referring to his stay at Gilbert Middleton's tavern in Annapolis the night before. He stayed in "New Town at Chester" on April 29 before embarking on a busy day of travel the next morning.

It is possible that Smith met with Washington during his brief stay, inviting him to Washington College's annual visitation in a few weeks; shortly after his visit, Smith sent Washington a formal invitation, without taking the niceties of re-acquaintance. Smith began grandly, in the manner of a public proclamation: "In the Name & Behalf of the Visitors & Governors of Washington College and by their Order… Visitation is to be held on Tuesday, May 18." More than anything, perhaps, Smith was seeking to impress his new college's board with the power to summon the most famous celebrity on the continent.

Smith informed Washington that "Gentlemen of the first Distinction from every County on the Eastern Shore" would be in attendance, and that his "Presence at some one Meeting… is an Honour, which they most earnestly wish for, as it would give the highest Sanction to the Institution & be truly animating to a numerous Body of youth." Smith went on to plead on behalf of the students—desperate to entertain Washington with a play called *The Tragedy of Gustavus Vasa, the Great Deliverer of Sweden from Danish Oppression*, also known in Dublin as *The Patriot*. They had rehearsed it so diligently that Smith felt comfortable enough to allow Washington to choose the day of his liking for the event, "either before or after the 18th." Smith even sent John Page, a trustee of the college, to hand-deliver the letter to Washington in Philadelphia.

NINTH VISIT: MAY 1784

While no written response from Washington survives, Smith must have received word from Page that the great man would return to Kent

County, for he postponed the visitation ceremonies until May 20—the day Washington passed through on his journey back to Mount Vernon. Washington apparently considered the act of affixing his name to the list of board of visitors and governors truly "trifling," because he never once mentioned it in his letters or diaries. On the other hand, Smith and his infant college would never *stop* mentioning it.

Washington College's longstanding efforts to publicize its relationship with the Father of His Country began with a published report that Smith commissioned later that year. *An Account of Washington College* vaguely described Washington's actions during the May visit, but gave more details of the honors bestowed on him. For example, it quoted the custom-written epilogue of *Gustavus* that the student performers added to the play:

> How late did fell Oppression, o'er this Land,
> With more than *Danish Fury* raise her Hand;
> When lo! A Hero of immortal Name
> From where *Potowmack* rolls his mighty Stream,
> Arose the Champion of his Country's Cause,
> The Friend of Mankind, Liberty and Laws;
> While in the Conflict Heaven and Earth engag'd
> And gave us PEACE, where *War* and Rapine rag'd.

It is likely that this verse had been composed by Dr. Smith and, in *An Account of Washington College*, the author (again, probably Smith) wrote that it "drew Tears of Gratulation from every Eye, and repeated Bursts of Applause from every Heart." (Including, one is meant to assume, the applause and tears of the most famous person on the campus green that day.) The visit was a great public-relations victory for Smith's small school.

* * *

BEFORE WASHINGTON'S NEXT VISIT to Chestertown, the Confederation's problems would boil over. Shay's Rebellion in Massachusetts was the first of several uprisings from Vermont to South Carolina. Congress had lost all hope for the current system of government and called for a convention to revise the Articles of Confederation. This led to the famous Constitutional Convention in Philadelphia, where the new government was born. Washington would soon be the unanimous choice as first president and the worldwide symbol of the new American system.

Still hard at work in Chestertown, William Smith was prepared to capitalize again on the popularity of Washington. Following the lead of other notable colleges, including Smith's old College of Philadelphia, the trustees of Washington College decided to grant Washington an honorary degree.

In an address sent to Washington on June 24, 1789, "actuated by the sincerest personal affection, as well as the purest public considerations," the officials congratulated Washington on his recent attainment of the presidency. "We cannot but recall to mind," they continued, "of our former address to you, and your benevolent answer to the same"—a reference to his having joined the board.

They continued to invoke their history with Washington, claiming that "amidst all the public monuments which your country sought to erect to you, even while *living*, none would be more acceptable than a Seminary of Universal learning...which had erected for you a monument in the heart of every good-Citizen." And referring to Washington's 1782 letter to Dr. Smith, when he had hoped "the period should arrive when we could hail the blest return of Peace," the trustees proclaimed, "The happy period is now arrived. ...This Seat of learning hath attained to such proficiency in the sciences, as to wait upon you with the promised *wreath of literary honor*; which we trust you will not reject, although from an Institution of inferior standing, yet not of inferior gratitude and affection to the chief of those which have already dignified themselves by presenting you with the like honors." In other words, although Harvard and Yale might have been more distinguished, they couldn't possibly love George more than Washington College.

The address was signed by Smith and accompanied by a diploma conferring the honorary degree of Doctor of Laws. Smith, accompanied by two members of the board, delivered it personally to the president in New York, then the nation's capital. Washington sent an official letter of thanks a few weeks later.

"Among the numerous blessings which are attendant on Peace," the president wrote, "may be reckoned the prosperity of Colleges and Seminaries of learning...It affords me peculiar pleasure to know that the seat of learning under your direction hath attained to such proficiency in the sciences since the peace." What is unclear is whether, apart from his "peculiar pleasure," Washington found amusement in the small rural college that made every effort to grab his attention.

TENTH VISIT: MARCH 1791
(THE CURSE IS BORN)

But George Washington's next experience with Kent County would be more peculiar than pleasurable. In 1791, having completed a tour of the Northeast, Washington set out on a Southern Tour as an opportunity to meet citizens south of Mount Vernon. Before the trip began, Washington had to travel from Philadelphia to his Potomac estate. He ended up taking his old route, passing through Chestertown for the first time as president.

The entourage that accompanied him was likely the largest he had ever brought through Kent County. (After all, he never did bring the Continental Army). Washington's diary states, "In this tour, I was accompanied by Major Jackson, my equipage, & attendance consisted of a Charriot & four horses drove in hand—a light baggage wagon and two horses—four saddle horses beside a led one for myself and five—to wit—my Valet de Chambre, two footmen, Coachman & postilion."

Washington left Philadelphia in the late morning of March 21. He stopped in Chester, Pennsylvania, and then Wilmington the next day. Washington had intended to go down the Western Shore of Maryland to Baltimore, but on the way to Wilmington found "the Roads very heavy—and receiving unfavorable Accts. of those between this place and Baltimore, determined to cross the Bay by the way of Rockhall."

Having never had much trouble on the water, Washington knew little of what the Chesapeake had in store for him this time.

On Wednesday, March 23, Washington reached Chestertown. He dined and lodged at Worrell's Tavern, which stood on the corner of Cannon and Queen Streets. (The building was torn down around 1900.) Two of his horses had fallen ill: his riding horse lost its appetite and another suffered "stiffness in all his limbs." While the president enjoyed himself, he sent one of his many servants ahead to Rock Hall to ready boats for departure at nine o'clock the next morning. Even the Revolutionary War naval veteran and Chestertown resident Captain James Nicholson went to Rock Hall to prepare for Washington's boat journey.

The next morning Washington left town at six o'clock, rode for three hours to Rock Hall, and ate breakfast there. A little after nine o'clock, the group hoped to leave but were severely delayed "for want of contrivance." Of the "two Boats in aid of the two Ferry Boats," not one was large enough to accommodate all of Washington's entourage and luggage. As it was getting late in the afternoon, Washington decided to fill the largest boat with as much as he could. He had to leave a servant and two horses behind when he finally departed at three o'clock.

But the delay was nothing compared to the events of the next twenty-four hours.

Washington's usually laconic diary becomes effusive, even melodramatic, in describing his crossing of the Chesapeake. The wind on the Bay was light until five o'clock, when it turned "stark calm" for another hour. As the sun was setting, a southwesterly wind picked up, slowly becoming a gale, and Washington's life was "in imminent danger, from the unskillfulness of the hands, and the dulness of [the boat's] sailing." At eight o'clock Washington's boat reached the mouth of the Severn River, leading to Annapolis, but his luck was not getting any better. It was dark, and thanks to "the ignorance of the People on board, with respect to navigation," the vessel ran aground on Greenbury Point. "With much exertion and difficulty," the boat got off, only to sail deeper into the darkness and gathering storm.

Washington describes the night as "immensely dark with heavy and variable squals of wind—constant lightning & tremendous thunder" made worse by the crew "having no knowledge of the Channel." The confluence of these factors grounded the ship again at Horne's Point. "Not knowing where [he] remained, not knowing what might happen," President Washington—the triumphant general who had brought the British war machine to its knees—nearly surrendered to a Maryland waterway.

The fifty-nine-year-old president spent the night in his "Great Coat & Boots, in a birth not long enough for me by the head, & much cramped." His servants, the crew and his horses spent the night without cover stuck in the Severn riverbed.

The boat was still stuck when the sun came up the next morning. Another vessel sailed by and picked up Washington and his baggage. He left his coachman behind to tend his horses and carriage until he could send another vessel to fetch them. Maryland Governor John Eager Howard honored Washington with parties and dinners in Annapolis to help him recover. Howard had actually set out the night before to meet Washington in Rock Hall but turned back due to the storm.

Rumors of Washington's ordeal circulated throughout tidewater Maryland. In its next issue, the *Maryland Gazette*, a popular Maryland newspaper, ran the story of "the chief treasure of America" and his Chesapeake adventure.

After an experience like that, why would Washington ever cross the Bay again? Royal commissions? Acts of Parliament? Political instabilities? No. Wild horses couldn't drag Washington back to the Eastern Shore.

* * *

ACCORDING TO SOME HISTORIANS—and to the Chestertown marker—Washington made a final visit in September 1793, after precipitously leaving Philadelphia for Mount Vernon in response to an outbreak of yellow fever. In his diary entry of September 10, Washington wrote, "Set out with my family for Mot. Vernon in Virginia."

Later that afternoon, Washington wrote to Secretary of State, Thomas Jefferson, about the "unpromising state of Negotiation at Madrid" in a letter dated at Chester—but given the timing, this must have been Chester, Pennsylvania. The letter did have an Eastern Shore reference, however. Mentioning the American chargé d'affaires in Spain, William Carmichael—born across the river from Chestertown at Round Top—Washington wrote, "Mr. Carmichael must not be the person left there, for, from him we should never hear a tittle of what is going forward at the Court of Madrid." Perhaps Washington thought that if a whole *crew* of Eastern Shore men could not steer a ferry, how could *one* hope to steer foreign policy?

But in fact, Washington had also been thinking kindly of the Eastern Shore that day. Before leaving Philadelphia that September morning, Washington wrote a letter to James Lloyd, the chairman of a meeting of Kent County residents. On September 1, Lloyd forwarded to Washington the unanimous resolutions passed on August 31, endorsing the president's proclamation of neutrality in the French war with Great Britain, Austria and Prussia.

Washington, who felt the proclamation was "preserving our peace," thanked the Kent County residents for their agreement. "'Tis by such a spirit that in any event we shall secure the internal tranquility of our Country, its respectability, and shall be enabled to encounter with firmness any attempt, hostile to its safety, its honor, or its welfare." Washington told the "respectable Citizens" of Kent County that their expressions of confidence and attachment towards myself…impress me with…their fervor and earnestness."

The "fervor and earnestness" of Kent County's attachment to Washington were probably what fabricated the story of the 1793 visit, because it never happened. The next day, Washington was in Elkton, Maryland—a stop on his way down the Western Shore.

In fact, not only would Washington never cross the county's threshold again, but neither would his next thirty successors. Then, in 1932, the marker honoring the nation's first president was erected in the center of town—and presto, the following year, Franklin Roosevelt finally visited, an event that made national newsreels. Poor little overlooked Chestertown was vindicated. After Truman and Eisenhower visited while in office, it seemed the curse was truly lifted.

But then again, it is now 53 years and counting since a sitting president has come to Kent County.

The Yule Log: Remembering Christmas in 18th-century Kent County

PEREGRINE WROTH

Editor's Note: Peregrine Wroth (1786-1879) composed the following essay in 1858 for his children. In it, he remembers Christmas as it was celebrated during his boyhood in Kent County at the end of the 18th century—not only by Wroth's family and their neighbors, but also by their African-American slaves. Especially fascinating is Wroth's description of customs and musical traditions that had been brought from Africa and melded with the European traditions of the season. And the latter part of his essay proves that lamentations over the crassness and commercialism of "modern" Christmas are not unique to our own time. "The Yule Log" is included in one of several handwritten volumes discovered by Washington College Professor Davy McCall and donated to the College Archives by Wroth's descendants. It was transcribed by Peter W. Knox '06. The footnotes to the essay are Wroth's own.

"THE YULE LOG." This phrase awakens the sleeping memories of good, old times in my Fatherland; and the near approach of the Great Christian Festival recalls to mind the long-lost customs which were brought to this country by the first Emigrants from England, and which mingled with and crowned the pleasures of Christmas in the days of my Boyhood.

Though the sad retrospect affects me almost to tears, I cannot throw it off, but memory clings to it with a fondness and yearning which can only be felt by those who lived at that time. The number of these is every year growing less and it cannot be long before the last link in the chain which connects that age with the present, will be broken, and disappear forever!

It was more than sixty[1] years ago. The third generation is now rising into manhood since there things were! Customs, manners—all things are changed! The contracted dimensions of the modern fire-place, with the finely sculptured, marble jambs and mantels, had not been seen. The ornamented grate and radiator had not been invented; and even the old tin-plate stove for the consumption of wood was only seen in the shops of the carpenter, the tailor and the shoemaker. The very existence of anthracite in the bowels of the Earth, where it had been hidden in long-lost ages by the Creator, had not been suspected! Parlour, dining room and kitchen were furnished with broad and deep fire-places in which large piles of wood crackled and blazed, and cast a strong heat and light to every corner of the room.

These fires blazed with peculiar lustre at Christmas. Before the dawn of the day so long desired and longed for, the younger members of the family (I am speaking of the family in the *country*) were up and astir. The young children had searched and emptied their stockings, which had been hung up the night before, of the good things annually supplied by good old Cris Kinkle (St Nicholas—the Patron Saint of young children). The capacious bowl of Egg-Nog was brewed; the hickory Yule Log sparkled and blazed on the ample hearth; the servants large and small with their shining ebony faces and teeth of pearl, peeped through the windows and half-opened doors, and all was prepared to salute the rising sun with the well-charged Christmas Gun.

As soon as he [the sun] appeared, the Ecchoes of the report were brought back from the surrounding woods, where the older servants—men and women—came back from the Quarter[2] dressed in their new suits of home-

---

[1] This was written in 1858.

[2] The house where the servants lived was so called.

made kersey, leading the children who could walk, and carrying in their arms those who could not, and entered the Great House[3] to receive their Christmas dram[4] at the hands of their master. I well remember that the children in the arms would turn off the glass without a wry-face.

This annual ceremony (daily through Christmas week) being over, the servants retired to the Quarter where they were regaled with a plentiful breakfast. This being dispatched, the Banjo, a musical instrument which they had brought with them from Africa, was introduced and the merry dance began with the well-remembered words:

Peregrine Wroth
circa 1810

> "Jack Butter in the fat
> Hop, and git over dat."

Here we will leave them awhile.

In the Great House, the Egg Nog was handed about, and all partook of the foaming beverage. After a breakfast of hot well-buttered Buckwheat cakes, rolls, and Biscuit, and sometimes with Johnny cake, and coffee, garnished with stuffed sausages, the family party began to assemble and dining room and Parlour were soon filled.

---

[3] The home of the master, so called by the servants.

[4] The Christmas *dram* was by them called their *Christmas.*

In the meantime the cooks were busy in preparing the Old Gobler for the spit, and the large Dinner pot, hanging over the fire, was filled with a delicious year-old ham and chines and other pork, with store of cabbage, potatos, turnips and other vegetables. Pot-pies of Goose or chicken were not forgotten, and ample provision had before been made of minced and pumpkin pies, plum-puddings and many other good things of that day.

While dinner was in preparation—to be served up at one o'clock, *never* later—the male members of the party, if the day was fine, whiled away the time by shooting at a target, or galloping round the neighbourhood, sipping their neighbours' Eggnog and romping with their daughters. Universal hilarity reigned throughout the country; but I can assure you, my dear children, that Intoxication—in *genteel* circles—was unknown. All was cheerful but sober—and a modest kiss was considered no breach of decorum! A sad countenance was nowhere seen; and if one had ventured to appear, it would soon have been laughed away.

Let us now pay another visit to the Quarter.

The Servants, who in *those primitive days*, thought no man in the country was so good or so grate a man as *Master*, and who never approached him without lifting the hat or scraping the ground with the toe of their shoes, had their full share of unrestrained mirth and jollity. In every family there was a "leader of all sports." In my Father's Quarter this leader was Cuffee—the only son of Aunt Dinah, my mother's chief cook and confidential servant in the Kitchen. He would place a large log in the front yard of the Quarter and boring a hole in it with an auger, fill it with water and plug it with a black coal from the fire-place. In the intervals of the song and the dance he would spring from the door of the Quarter and striking a heavy blow with an axe on the hole in the log, jump high in the air and striking his feet together three times before reaching the ground utter a loud shout as an echo to the report from the log almost as loud as that of a gun. He would then return to his comrades and give out a line of his unpremeditated song—to be answered by them in full chorus. The rhythm of their songs was such

as that in Africa at this day, and was thence introduced into this country.
I give a specimen—

Leader: "Work away, my brave boys."
Chorus: "So – ho!"
Leader: "Husk up the man's corn."
Chorus: "So – ho!" (prolonged)

Not only at Christmas, but at the night husking matches in the different neighbourhoods, the leader would go on half the night, improvising his song and promising his comrades plenty of pork, pot pye and cider when the heap of corn was husked. Cuffee was the leader generally at these nightly meetings, as he was admired for his *poetic* talent. And he would often exhibit feats of agility which would astonish the clowns and merry-andrews of the modern circus.

I give another specimen of a chorus (the *song* is forgotten) to one of his most admired efforts—

"Raccoon foot and 'possum tail
New Town[5] gals will never fail."

Those days of homely[6] sport and kind and cordial feelings, unadulterated by admixture with modern fashions, recur like a remembered dream! And I recall not only the plain but substantial fare and good cheer, the house and field sports of both masters and servants, but also the many evidences of the superior social enjoyment of those *now* forgotten days, the cordial greetings, the interchange of true home-bred feelings, the genuine, unsophisticated welcome given to guests, with a sad pleasure!

When a dance was got up, there were no French bows and grimaces; no French rigadoons and chassees; no French minuettes and Pirouettes; but the plain, honest jigs and hornpipes of Anglo-Saxon birth; no airs or

---

[5] Chester Town, then recently built, was, by all, known by the name of New Town.

[6] Homely – home-like, plain, not *ugly*.

politeness (falsely so called), no outside blandness intended to conceal the feelings of the heart; but true heart-felt and *heart-reaching* plainness of salutation which could not be misinterpreted!

That there is more Scientific culture of the present day, is not denied; but the culture is that of the *head*, not of the *heart*; a culture in which all cordial feeling is repudiated. *Home*, with all its thousand attractions, its swelling, gushing, perennial fountains of enjoyment, is not now the place where the young seek for pleasure, but the Oyster house and hotel! And the house-hold and home-bred sympathies which once clustered around the family hearth are now dried up and withered by the sirocco breath of a cold, all-absorbing selfishness! Who, with such memories thronging about him, would not mourn over the retrospect and long for the return of good old times?

In the projects and customs of the present day, the heart is not consulted. Self- interest has usurped the place once occupied by the Law of Kindness; and in all family and neighbourhood intercourse, tinsel and glitter and glare and outside show, reign supreme!

You perceive, my dear children, that I am earnest on this subject; and I do not hesitate to add my firm conviction that, in all that relates to the social conditions of the Past and the Present, the latter is not an improvement on the former. There is more learning now, but less true wisdom! More external polish of manners, but much less *heartiness* and *sincerity*; more wealth and infinitely less generosity and openhanded and openhearted liberality!

I could continue on in this strain for another sheet or more, but this may suffice to show my sincere testimony in favour of the good old time of long-buried generations!

At the turn of the 20th century, the wooden truss Chester River Bridge provided a swing bridge to allow boats to pass through.

The brick path along the dirt road leading to Washington College became known as "Lovers' Walk."

The firehouse on Cross Street, built in 1899, had been turned into a storefront by 1938. Gill Bros. dairy was next door.

A customer pauses outside G. H. Robinson's on Cross Street in pre-1922 Chestertown. In its later incarnation as Gill Bros. ice cream parlor, the storefront (now home of Play It Again Sam's) was a favorite local haunt.

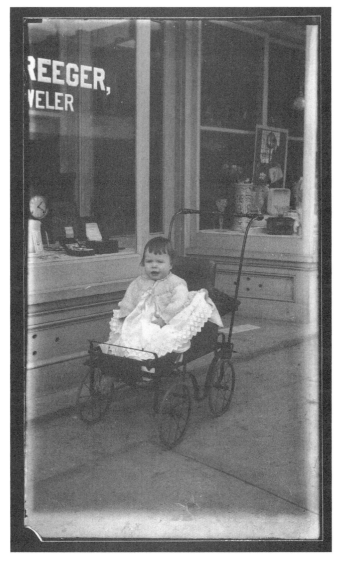

A Chestertown toddler travels in style at the turn of the 20th century.

The 18th-century building now known as the Custom House was erected next to the original Custom House, which did not survive.

Wide Hall, a finely-executed home in the Georgian style, was built by Thomas Smythe, a merchant and shipbuilder, circa 1770. The dormered hip roof was restored shortly after 1905 when Mr. and Mrs. W. W. Hubbard acquired the house.

Emmanuel Church, an early Anglican Church, hosted the first convention which proposed and adopted the name "Protestant Episcopal Church." The bell tower was added in 1905.

The Lusby House on High Street was built by local carpenter William O. Smith and sold to Richard Smyth in 1860, and eventually acquired by the Lusbys in 1885. Among the first Chestertonians to own a car, the Lusbys provided taxicab service between Tolchester and Chestertown.

PHOTO: TYLER CAMPBELL

In this 1984 photo, Vince Raimond (left) and Jack Schroeder get into character for the Chestertown Tea Party Reenactment, a street festival they organized to commemorate a local revolt purportedly held in the spring of 1774.

PHOTO: TYLER CAMPBELL

Carroll Gibbs, one of Chestertown's most memorable characters, demonstrated tremendous civic pride in keeping our streets clean.

Leo Hicks and Nubby Taylor ran a machine shop and junk yard on Cannon Street.

If Cooper's Hardware Store on High Street didn't have it, you didn't need it.

PHOTO TYLER CAMPBELL

The old jail, built in 1884, stood next to the Court House. It was demolished in 1988.

PHOTO TYLER CAMPBELL

Taking The Boat Downriver

KATHY WAGNER

Waiting for the sun
like a weak old back burner
on an electric stove
to light back up to high
again, we could sleep
completely through winter.
But somewhere in the middle
of the river's hole
I give in to the slowness
of my soul and climb into my
wooden boat bundled up
in barnacles and a veil
of mold and head downstream
to Long Cove. I hug
the shoreline like a blind
seamstress stitching
the salvaged edge of a dress
of gold, and try to keep
as I've been told exactly
one half-inch to the interior.
The repetition of the pointing
of the bow into the waves
wakens the morning's

saws and I hear the diagonal
flight of wayward geese
cutting across the bight
as I follow time to save time
in a dream of having
nowhere to go. I raise my arms
to carry the fog, the sky's
basket of clothes, then touch
the folds of dress and down,
without their threads
or bones, as if without this body
I must now head home.

Black Patriots on the Eastern Shore

ELIZABETH CLAY

THE AUTUMN AIR was crisp and fresh and, as the fallen leaves blew across the tobacco and wheat fields of Kent County, a wind of change was also stirring for the African Americans of the Eastern Shore. It was 1863. Union military steamships were sailing up the many rivers of the Chesapeake, coming to recruit slaves off plantations for the Army of the Potomac. This development was to complicate the already complex political fabric in Maryland, whose residents were torn between loyalty to the North or South. The hundreds of slaves who left Kent County with memories of bondage fresh in their minds returned two years later as heroes—at least to friends and families if not to all their white neighbors and former owners. Their story of wartime heroism and postwar pride is one of the little-known secrets of Chestertown's history.

A surviving monument to that story is a ramshackle old building that still stands on South Queen Street: the Charles Sumner Post of the Grand Army of the Republic. Once back from war, these veterans established their own chapter of the veterans' organization to remember their service and unite to help each other. While it is unclear now what the reception was for black veterans once back in Chestertown, the fact that their G.A.R. post took on the assignment of honoring veterans—both black and white—of the Civil War on Decoration Day, shows that the black veterans cared enough to honor all veterans. The black veterans also were able to establish a strong community for themselves through the Post where they not only held meetings, but also had family gatherings.

For many years, the contribution of African Americans to the history of Kent County was overlooked. In Monument Park in Chestertown, there is a Civil War monument honoring a few dozen white Confederate and Union troops from Kent County. Unbeknownst to most is that more than 400 African-American soldiers from Kent County also fought for the Union—and more than one-third of them perished in the process. (It took until the late 1990s to erect a monument in their honor.) Even lesser known are the stories of the individual men who fought. But by examining long-forgotten military records, newspapers and courthouse documents, it is possible to reconstruct the lives of some of the black soldiers and to tell the story of their postwar lives as veterans.

Following the Emancipation Proclamation in 1863, Lincoln sent an order that African Americans could participate in segregated Union army regiments. Because Maryland was a slave state, yet still part of the Union, this order applied to enslaved African Americans on Maryland plantations—since they were not considered free under the Emancipation Proclamation. Thus in late 1863, steamers carrying recruiters traveled up the Chesapeake Bay and established recruitment stations. One such station was located in Chestertown. Recruiters also visited the local plantations of large slave owners and offered the owners a bounty of up to $300 per slave for their enlistment in the war. If the owner refused, he was considered disloyal and the slaves were seized anyway. The recruitment of slaves caused much excitement and dismay on the Eastern Shore. A notice in the *Cecil Democrat* in October reported a "stampede." The paper said, "[A]about 150 negroes left the lower part of this county on Tuesday night last. About forty were met on Wednesday morning between the head of Sassafras and Galena, going in the direction of the latter place, probably toward some appointed rendezvous below."

The *Kent County News* also reported the effect of recruitment in its September and October issues of 1863. On September 19, the *News* commented that Col. Birney had been allowed to form a regiment in Maryland and the newspaper was "pained" to report that slaves were going to be a part of the military. The paper said that allowing slaves to serve was a violation of a Maryland law that punished anyone who helped slaves to leave their owners. The article consisted mainly of a rant against the enlistment of slaves and it asked the question, "Can the Government permit its officers to violate the Constitution and laws of a loyal State?" The article questioned why, after giving support, loyalty and cooperation to the Union, Maryland "is now to have her slaves taken, her crops left ungathered, her grounds unploughed...deprived of her very means of subsistence...her people brought to suffering for her patriotism and sacrifices in the cause of their country!"

But on the same page of the paper was a statement that contradicted the argument. The paper announced that according to *The Baltimore American*, the "colored troops raised in this State are to be credited to the quota of Maryland." In other words, because the enlistment of black troops was moving along so quickly, the impending draft ordered by the Lincoln Administration would probably not be enforced in Maryland, thus saving many white men from having to serve involuntarily.

An article in the next issue of the *Kent County News*, "The Abduction of Slaves from Our County," described a steamboat that went to Eastern Neck Island to take away slaves for the army. The slaves apparently knew that the boat was coming and were waiting for it, but there were so many of them that not all could be taken. The author of the article was "unable to express the feeling of indignation and of mortification that these proceedings have aroused among all classes of the community." Clearly, the disruption caused on the Eastern Shore by the recruitment of slaves was significant and was perceived as unfair to the people who needed slaves for their plantations to operate. The following week, the *Kent County News* reported on the qualifications necessary for black people to serve in the military. They could serve if: they were free and volunteered, if they were slaves of a "rebel" or someone disloyal and they volunteered to enlist, or if they had consent from their owners. It was further reported that all slaves volunteered by their masters or of disloyal masters would be free after their service, and loyal masters would receive a bounty for their slaves. The last notice was that colored troops would receive "…clothing, rations, and ten dollars per month. Three dollars per month will be deducted for clothing." On the same page of the newspaper, it was reported that officers under Col. Birney went to Chestertown and recruited 300 slaves. This, according to the *News*, brought the total number of slaves taken from Kent County to 400. The article states that many slave owners were left "without a single serviceable hand" and that "in some instances boys, much too small for soldiers, were permitted to go away, but so far as our knowledge extends negro women were uniformly refused."

In the same issue of the paper is a third mention of the recruitment of black troops. In an excerpt of an article from *The National Intelligencer*, a visitor from Washington, DC, commented on the situation on the Eastern Shore. This "intelligent resident" declares that the "ruthless abduction of the able-bodied slaves so essential to the agricultural operations of the Eastern Shore…" must stop immediately. With all the men gone, the slave women and children were left for their masters to feed and care for, but none of the men were there to work the farms.

In the next week's paper of October 10, there is a final mention of the issue of slave enlistment in an article announcing "Enlistment of Slaves in Maryland Suspended." The taking of Maryland slaves had been stopped because the lack of servitude had caused farmers to suffer, and there was no new labor to replace the lost slaves.

It was not long before the 400 black Kent County troops—along with nearly 8,000 from the rest of the state—found themselves at the front lines of the war—and in one of its most notorious actions. The Battle of the Crater at Petersburg, Virginia, on July 30, 1864, was a dark day for many African-American soldiers, including twenty from Kent County who were killed. The original Union strategy for the battle was to plant a mine under the Confederate line. This mine would kill any Confederates near it, as well as open up the Confederate defenses. When the mine was detonated on the morning of July 30, it opened a massive crater in the battlefield and killed a few hundred Confederates. Union Major General Ambrose E. Burnside ordered a division of the United States Colored Troops (USCT) to lead the Union troops around the edges of the crater to attack the disorganized Confederates. Major General George Meade, one of the commanders of the Army of the Potomac, was against this plan, fearing that if the attack failed many black troops would be killed, and it would cause outrage in the North. Burnside agreed to change his plan and have white soldiers go in first, but the order came too late and the white troops were not trained as to what they should do, causing disorder and disaster. The white troops, instead of going around the crater, went directly into it, where the Confederates could easily shoot down at them. Burnside was determined and, in the heat of the moment, rather than give up, he sent the black troops into the crater, where they were relentlessly shot at for hours as they tried to escape. At the close of the battle, about 5,300 Union soldiers had been slaughtered, half of whom were black.

Besides death in combat, twenty-five percent of the soldiers died from disease and many more had recurring medical problems once they returned home. Fifteen percent of the black enlistees from Kent County served in the Navy, the only unsegregated part of the Civil War military.

After returning to Kent County at the close of the Civil War, twenty-eight African-American veterans established a G.A.R. post in Chestertown in 1882. This post was named the Charles Sumner G.A.R. Post #25, after the prominent Massachusetts abolitionist; it was the twenty-fifth post in Maryland. In 1908, the group moved into the building on Queen Street which was to be their headquarters until 1950.

The purpose of the G.A.R. post was to promote patriotism and allow the comrades to bond and help their less fortunate brethren. The members collected dues at their weekly meetings and paid medical and funeral bills for the families of veterans. The national G.A.R. was one of the few integrated social institutions in 19th-century America. In Maryland, the G.A.R. had separate black and white posts but was never officially segregated, and they were all part of the Maryland G.A.R. The black members were able to participate in all activities of the G.A.R., and they all marched at the same time at statewide and national events, although sometimes separately. African-American posts were established in Maryland directly following the Civil War and made up about one-third of the Maryland G.A.R., with a considerable number of posts on the Eastern Shore. But Chestertown had no white G.A.R. post, and the Sumner Post had no white members—a fact that indicates much about politics and race relations in town after the Civil War.

According to Barbara Gannon, a scholar of black veterans' groups, the Charles Sumner Post had an impressive lifespan and must have been a very important part of the Kent County African-American community. In 1929 the post was still active, as were only three other African-American posts in Maryland. As Gannon observes, the fact that the members owned their hall is also an important sign of the significance of the post.

The duty of honoring all veterans every year was upheld by the members of the Charles Sumner Post on May 30—Decoration Day, later called Memorial Day. It was described many times in the *Kent County News*. Members of the Post first observed the day in 1883. One news report reads, "Decoration Day was observed in Chestertown last Wednesday by 'Charles Sumner Post' No. 25, G.A.R., numbering twenty-eight members (colored)…The Post, headed by the Oriental Brass Band, Geo. Carmichael leader, marched from Perkins' Hall to Janes Church Cemetery, and there decorated the graves of [black soldiers]…Ceremonies were read by the officers and each grave was strewn with flowers and salutes fired. The Post then marched to Chester Cemetery and performed the same ceremonies over the graves of all the deceased soldiers known to be resting there, and from thence marched back to the hall and were dismissed…In the evening services were continued at the hall by the decoration of that building and the delivery of addresses by Wm. Perkins, J.A. Jones, and Fred Nichols, and closing with refreshments served to all the large number present."

Each year in a similar fashion, members of the Charles Sumner Post honored the deceased soldiers who served from Kent County, black and white alike. In fact, in 1889 the *Kent News* confessed that "the sacred duty of honoring the memory of those who died in defense of our country, or who having survived the misfortunes of war have since fallen by the wayside, seems to devolve entirely upon the colored people of our town. At least they are the only ones who observe the day in Chestertown. The annual sermon to Sumner Post was preached at Janes M.E. Church...On Thursday Sumner Post, four wagons decorated with flowers, and the Oriental and Calvert bands paraded our streets and decorated the graves of both white and colored. At night seven memorial addresses were made at Perkins' Hall."

The meetings of the Charles Sumner Post were conducted in the meeting room, which was located on the second floor of the Post so that no one could spy on them. (The door also had a peephole, which still exists.) Reports filed by the national organization's inspectors reveal that all of the Chestertown veterans were fully outfitted with G.A.R. uniforms, differing slightly from Civil War military uniforms.

FROM PENSION RECORDS and other documents, it is possible to discover many interesting details about the lives of various members.

One of the founders, George Dumpson, was a slave when he enlisted in the Army. His owner, John Lusby, received $200 for Dumpson's service in the Seventh Maryland regiment, Company D. Dumpson was twenty-five years old, six feet tall, described as having black eyes and curly hair, and born in Kent County. He enlisted September 26, 1863 for three years and was taken to Birney's Barracks in Baltimore to be mustered in. In order to receive payment, John Lusby filled out an application for compensation and gave Dumpson a deed of manumission. In one of the documents, John Lusby agreed that "I, my heirs, executors, or assigns, shall never hereafter make or enforce any claim to the labor or services of said slave; and pledge myself to execute a valid Deed of Manumission and Release of all my claims to service forever of said George Dumpson." In the documents, Lusby also disclosed that he owned George's mother and that is how he came to have George as a slave.

Lusby is present in the public records of Kent County. In the 1860 census of Chestertown, a seventy-one-year-old John Lusby is listed with his much younger wife, thirty-eight-year-old Elizabeth Lusby, and their four young children. Lusby was very wealthy for the times with $18,000 worth of real estate, and $4,500 in other assets. In the

1860 Slave Schedules for Kent County, Lusby is listed as owning five slaves between the ages of fourteen and twenty-two—two females and three males. The twenty-two-year-old black male is most likely George Dumpson.

In the 1870 census George Dumpson was listed as residing with the Simon Wickes family and working as a farm hand. It seems common from the Chestertown censuses that after the Civil War, black people moved in with white families to work as cooks, farm laborers and domestics. For instance, living next door to Simon Wickes was Joseph Ringgold, another prominent white Chestertown resident. After his family of four is listed, nine black people are listed, most of them farm hands and the three females having the titles of cook, house girl and nurse.

In the 1880 census, George Dumpson appears in the fourth district of Kent County with his wife, Catharine. He is listed as a thirty-five-year-old mulatto male farm laborer who cannot read or write. In his household are also residing three young children between five and ten, and a farm laborer. By this time in Chestertown, most of the African Americans seem to have established their own separate community, while ten years before, the African Americans were more mixed with whites, as they were before the war.

One interesting member of the Chestertown G.A.R. was Oscar James Crozier, a member of the drum corps of the Fifty-fourth Massachusetts, the historic African-American regiment depicted in the film *Glory*. He was born in Philadelphia and enlisted at Boston, but then moved to Kent County after the war and is buried in Janes Cemetery in Chestertown. He is listed as having been free on or before April 19, 1861. He was wounded in the eye on July 20, 1864 in Florida and may have been in Philadelphia's Eastern State Penitentiary in 1870, according to census records. In his pension application, he states that he has a "slight effect" in his left eye received in the line of duty in 1864 and an injury in his back received the same year.

Henry Mays and Charles Linsey appeared before a Notary Public in Kent County to provide testimony for Crozier. The pension application reads, "Henry Mays an Honorable Man of Chestertown 70 years old and made oath in Due Form Yes Sir I Have Known Oscar J. Crozier Ever Since Shortly after the Civil War He came to Kent County and Lived Down in Quaker Neck With a Mr. Walto for over Twenty years then He came to Live in Chestertown and married Mary Elizabeth Harris. No Sir He never was married Before He married Her. Yes Sir I Have Known Him to Run around With other Women and Have Known him Intimately Since Shortly after He came Here after the war."

In this document of an interview with people who knew Oscar Crozier it can be gleaned that he was a bit of a womanizer, but it is shown that he was never married before his current marriage. As with most of the affidavits in the pension files of Sumner vets, those testifying have their accounts written down for them, and then they make their marks. This affidavit however is written more like an interview.

In eighty-seven-year-old Charles Linsey's similarly conducted affidavit, he states many of the same facts, "No Sir He Was Never married But once He lived in my section of the Neck for over Twenty years and used to go With Different Women But When He married He had moved in Chestertown and He Courted and married Mary Elizabeth Harris This is His only wife by marriage Lots of Colored People used to Live with Each other." Linsey describes how African Americans were never fully recognized as being married but that Crozier and Mary Harris were married by the courts. On Oscar Crozier's death certificate, it says that he died from cardiac asthma and that he is buried in Chestertown; his grave, adorned with plastic flowers, is still visited by someone today.

In the pension records of various Sumner Post vets, there are many affidavits that they each provided for one another to prove each other's illnesses and need for pension money. Nelson Reed was a corporal in the Thirtieth Maryland Regiment, Company E, and helped to found the Sumner Post. In his pension application, a fellow private in the same company and of Chestertown, Joseph Cotton, testifies that he "was sick with measles at same time Nelson Reed was and was treated with him at Hospital at same time, that the said Nelson Reed suffered greatly with pain in back, limbs and head, and was very badly affected for three weeks. I know these facts from personal observation, being a comrade of the said Nelson Reed, and an eye witness at the time." In 1914 when Nelson's widow, Rachel, applied for widow's pension, the seventy-three-year-old Edward Miller, another veteran of the post, and his wife, Arimita Miller, testified for Rachel.

Edward Miller's affidavit provides the only mention I found of the Charles Sumner Post. He says that he has been acquainted with the couple for fifty years, asserting: "I knew him before he entered service and since has been associated with him in church and a comrade in Charles Sumner Post G.A.R. ...of the State of Maryland and he has resided in this town all his life from about the age of 25 yrs and I was a witness to his marriage and attended his burial." Nelson Reed apparently was unable to tell the pension office his age as there was no record. He wrote a letter to them to explain and also describes how he ended up in Kent County. He said, "I lived in Virginia my birth state and my mother had record of births in bible and I was told at the election of Buckhanan I was 25 yr. old. At the breaking out of the war I ran away from Va. And joined some regiment known as the Home Guards...I was sent to Kent County...then I enlisted and never went to Va. my home again until 1900: after reaching home found all my people deceased and found no trace of anything, they thinking I was deceased. While in Va. I inquired as to my age I found some playmates (white) and they put my age then as they supposed to be about 70 or 71; while I do not think I am old as they say yet I do claim 75 or 76." This tragic story suggests that Nelson Reed was possibly a slave in Virginia and ran away in order to fight. Unfortunately, his family never learned of his participation in the army.

Nelson Reed appears in the census in Chestertown after the war. In the 1870 census, Reed is a thirty-year-old black man born in Virginia who cannot read or write. His wife, Rachel, is twenty-five and keeps the house. They have three children, Mary, Henry and Daniel, each who attended school within the year, and he is listed as a boarder on Calvert Street with Rachel Miller. In 1900, Nelson Reed is still living on Calvert Street. He is sixty-three and his job is hauling lumber.

Henry Worrell, a soldier in Company D of the Seventh Regiment, was born in 1835, something proved by the court of Kent County, MD.

A court justice of Kent County said that by the last will and testament of Catharine H. Wroth "…late of Kent County deceased, bearing date the 27 Dec 1854 and duly proved and recorded in this office it appears that a negro man named Harry, alias Harry Worrell the bearer hereof is freed from slavery and further certify that it has been proved by satisfactory testimony that said Harry, alias Harry Worrell is the identical negro freed as aforesaid…Harry has a scar on his left cheek." Henry was injured at Petersburg in 1864 as he was carrying logs with a fellow comrade who let go of his end and "threw the whole weight of it upon me." It was an injury from which he never recovered. He said he never went to the doctor but treated himself with different liniments and was unable to work because of his injuries.

In the 1880 census for Chestertown, Henry Worrell is living with Joseph Wickes on High Street and is listed as a servant who works as a sailor. In 1900, Henry and his wife, Sophia, are living on Queen Street in their own household. Henry was born in 1838 and is a hostler, according to the census.

Most of the Sumner Post vets rented or owned their own homes by 1880 and were a part of the African-American community of Chestertown. This illustrates the *de facto* segregation that occurred more and more after Reconstruction. The races preferred to establish their own separate facilities.

Frederick Nichols, another founding member of the Post, seems to have made a successful life for himself after the war, as in his will he describes two properties, one located on Princess Street. His will also reveals that he owned a gold watch, organ, parlor furniture, dining room furniture, chinaware and books. He divided his personal estate among all his children and grandchildren.

The last surviving veteran, William Wesley Broadway, was eighty years old in 1930 and died March 17, 1931. He was buried in Janes Church Cemetery on March 22, 1931. A private in the Seventh Regiment, Company A, he was nineteen when he enlisted, according to his military records. He was described as five feet six inches, with black eyes and curly hair. He was born in Queen Anne's County on September

23, 1844, and enlisted there for three years on September 23, 1863. In the September and October 1863 records, he is listed as absent because he was "detached on recruiting service in St. Mary's County." Clearly, as soon as he enlisted, he was used to help recruit other slaves into the military. He married Mary Dunn in 1915 in Chestertown. His previous wife was Martha Woodland, from whom Broadway separated before she died in 1896. In the March 18, 1931 edition of *The Enterprise*, there is a small notice of the death of Wesley Broadway in the "News on the Run" section. This states, "Wesley Broadway, well known colored citizen, of Chestertown, died here today. Broadway is thought to be the last of the G.A.R. organization which once flourished in Kent. Death was due to pneumonia." By the time of Broadway's death, the Sumner Post was much less active than it had been in previous decades; Wesley Broadway's death closed the most important chapter of the Post's history. When he died, he took with him the last memories of a member of the Post.

After the last comrade died, families of the vets continued to use the Post for meetings and rented the building out for social events. The Haughton Brothers, a jazz group from Chestertown, performed there, as did Ella Fitzgerald in 1938 and the Chick Webb Orchestra. In 1950, the descendants of the G.A.R. veterans sold the hall to a fraternal association called the Centennial Lodge. The preamble to the Centennial Lodge Constitution stated that it was their mission to "soothe the sorrows and soften the pillows of the sick and dry up the tears of the children." But by 1985, the lodge had been abandoned and the former G.A.R. building fell into serious disrepair.

Today there are plans to restore this historic building so that its legacy can be preserved and its former glory can be honored. In its walls rests much of Kent County's post-Civil War history and doubtless many secrets of the G.A.R. The lives of the Sumner Post veterans are a testament to their success at finding a niche for themselves when they returned from the war to live among the whites, their former owners in some cases. Their stories add to the already varied history of Chestertown, and demonstrate the richness of the African-American community's past. Tidbits can be gleaned about the lives of the veterans who held meetings at the Charles Sumner Post, G.A.R. #25, but only the old Post building on Queen Street knows the truth.

Fred and Ginger—and Colonel Brown

P.J. WINGATE

ALTHOUGH IT NURTURES its artists to a degree unrivaled by most towns of its size, Chestertown is not so well known for contributions to the performing arts. Nevertheless, it was a local boy and Washington College graduate who became the impresario credited with a vital role in creating the most celebrated dance team in the history of theatre—Fred Astaire and Ginger Rogers.

This was Hiram S. Brown, Class of 1900, and later president of the movie firm RKO, which produced the first Astaire-Rogers film, *Flying Down to Rio*, and subsequently made millions of dollars from a series of movies by this most gifted pair of dancers. Colonel Brown, as he was known throughout most of his adult life, was no longer president of RKO when most of these later movies were produced. But it took no great foresight for Brown to see that they had an artistic diamond necklace and a financial gold mine in the dance team of Ginger Rogers and Fred Astaire.

Both Rogers and Astaire had played in Broadway shows and had minor roles in movies before they made their first film together, but neither was even close to being called a star when Hiram Brown brought them together in 1933. Even then the listed stars for *Flying Down to Rio* were Gene Raymond and Dolores Del Rio, both of whom have long since vanished into the mists of obscurity along with the plot of the movie itself.

Not so for Rogers and Astaire. They shot into the theatrical sky like rockets, propelled by their own incomparable talents and by Vincent Youmans, who provided the music they danced to: "The Carioca," "Orchids in the Moonlight," "Music Makes Me," and the title song, "Flying Down to Rio." In all subsequent movies they made together, Ginger Rogers and Fred Astaire were the stars, and their dancing became artistic treasures.

The story of the man who brought them together, Hiram Staunton Brown, is not well known even on the campus of his *alma mater*, despite the fact that he was chairman of the Board of Governors of the College from 1922 until 1950, longer than any other man in the history of the College to date. Brown was born at Quaker Neck in Kent County in 1882, and graduated *magna cum laude* from Washington College in 1900, at 18 years of age. He always was a leader on the campus, according to Judge T. Alan Goldsborough, who was a year ahead of Brown.

Judge Goldsborough was in a mellow mood in 1949 when he came back for his fiftieth class reunion, and one of his topics when he spoke at breakfast that day was Colonel Hiram S. Brown, chairman of the Board of Visitors and Governors, who was in the audience. "Staunton Brown was a year behind me," Judge Goldsborough said, "but he was the big man on campus even as a junior. He looked like a young, handsome Winston Churchill and he had that same bulldog jaw. He got elected president of just about everything and he always brought the prettiest girl in town to the dances. I hated him."

The Judge and Colonel Brown both smiled at that last remark, but Goldsborough may really have meant what he said because Hiram Brown did excite strong emotions on the part of his associates.

After graduation, Brown went to New York City where he worked briefly as a reporter for *The New York Times*, and then went into banking and business. During World War I he was a military finance officer, and that experience, followed by his later service in the National Guard, won him the title of Colonel, by which he was known from then on.

After the war he quickly developed the reputation in New York circles of being a hard-driving businessman and in 1924 he became president of the U.S. Leather Company, a large old prosperous firm headquartered in New York City. In 1928, while U.S. Leather was booming, RKO was a struggling theatre and movie company with a profit margin below what the directors thought it should be, so they persuaded Brown to leave U.S. Leather to become head of RKO. Brown made this change on January 1, 1929, less than a year before the stock market crashed and started the Great Depression.

The Depression prevented RKO from showing the kind of profitability that U.S. Leather had shown, and in fact it hovered on the brink of bankruptcy. Those who had been passed over at RKO, in favor of Brown, blamed all the company's trouble on him and cited his lack of experience in the theatre to support their claims. Actually, Brown was not as much a greenhorn in the theatre as his prior job might suggest. He had been living in New York City for many years and knew the theatre well, both as a customer and as a businessman. Also, he had never lost that eye for a pretty girl, which Judge Goldsborough mentioned, so when he saw Ginger Rogers on the stage in *Girl Crazy*, he had his agents sign her to a movie contract with RKO. Then when he got Fred Astaire under contract also, he was ready for *Flying Down to Rio*, which saved RKO from bankruptcy. The subsequent Astaire-Rogers movies made RKO one of the most profitable movie concerns of the decade, but that came after Brown had left RKO, following a series of battles with his subordinates.

One of these subordinates was Max Gordon, who later became famous as a producer of Broadway shows. In his memoirs, called *Max Gordon Presents,* Gordon tells how he and Brown clashed and who won that battle.

One of Gordon's responsibilities at RKO was the supervision of the 700 theatres in the Keith-Albee Orpheum circuit, which then made up a major part of RKO. Gordon was responsible not only for the theatres but also for the selection and scheduling of the vaudeville teams, which were then at least as important as the movies in selling tickets to the theatres. Gordon several times disagreed with Brown concerning these actors, singers and dancers. Then one day, not long after Brown took over, Gordon went on a tour of the theatres to see how and what they were doing. When he returned he found that his desk was gone from his office, which had been filled with buckets, brooms and mops.

Highly indignant, Gordon marched over to Brown's office and asked: "What does this all mean?"

"It means," Brown replied, "that you are out." And he was. The bull-dog jaw that Judge Goldsborough mentioned must have been set hard.

Max Gordon later proved by a long series of Broadway hits that his own judgment in matters of the theatre was good, but he never produced a show that came close to matching the financial success of the Rogers-Astaire dance team brought together by Colonel Brown.

Hiram Brown died at his home at Godlington Manor, near Chestertown, on May 4, 1950.

The Uptown Club: In the Days When Ray Charles, Otis Redding, B.B. King, Fats Domino, Little Richard and James Brown Hung Out Right Here in River City

LESLIE PRINCE RAIMOND

Editor's Note: Pearl Johnson Hackett, her daughter Sylvia Hackett Frazier and their cousin, Rosie Perkins Herbert, grew up just a few steps from the Uptown Club, Charlie Graves' popular venue for black musical artists in the 1950s and '60s. The club on the northwest corner of College Avenue and Calvert Street, though smaller than Harlem's Apollo Theatre and Chicago's Regal Theatre, was a popular stop for black artists performing on the Chitlin' Circuit—a loose network of jook joints, nightclubs, dance halls, bars, theatres and restaurants that flourished throughout the U.S. and especially in the South during the pre-Civil Rights era. Because of recording industry apartheid, which relegated black music to black audiences, black spaces and midnight-to-dawn time slots on radio, the Chitlin' Circuit was critical to the economic survival of black artists who had not crossed over to mainstream audiences.

ROSIE: Charlie's was the entertainment spot of the Eastern Shore... and the Western Shore. I can remember an influx of people coming from Wilmington, and Philadelphia, however the word got out, and this would be a crowded little town.

PEARL: When he had dances the cars were parked everywhere. You had to dress to go out!

ROSIE: I'm going back in the era when the Nike Base was first built, and the soldiers started coming, and you had to dress up. And the ladies really looked good. They had their hairdos; they worked all week to get an outfit for the weekend...

PEARL: .... to go down to Charlie's ....Because it was a popular place. You didn't wear your work-clothes to go there.

SYLVIA: Back when I could remember, Mr. Charlie Graves used to wear a suit every day, with a big brimmed hat, and a tie... Because he was the owner of the Uptown Club!

PEARL: We can go back to when Charlie had only the restaurant across the street. That was first. It was across the street, on the right-hand side. And then he went across the street and built a bar and dance hall. It must have been in the early '50s.

SYLVIA: I always thought it was an old saloon...as little kids; we'd walk past and peek in...

ROSIE: I remember first hearing about B.B. King coming to town... and then Fats Domino, and this is in the era of them first starting, getting on the Chitlin' Circuit. When stars came to town, I guess it got too hot in the building, and he would open the back doors and everybody would stand there and SEE the stars. If you weren't old enough to go to the show, you still got to see them.

SYLVIA: Even Etta James was here.

ROSIE: And the Franklin Girls—Aretha, Erma and one named Carolyn I think.

SYLVIA: You could almost say that from the James Brown-B. B. King era all of them have at least dropped in. Even Richard Prior.

ROSIE: Gene Chandler, Sam Cook, Clyde McPhatter, The Platters, Duke of Earl....

LESLIE: Otis Redding?

ROSIE: Yes! Otis Redding! It was just THAT POPULAR. They didn't have a showcase, and they weren't getting paid much on that Chitlin' Circuit. But it was a wonderful time. I remember seeing Ray Charles and Charlie always together like bosom buddies, and people saying "there go two Charles." Charlie Graves would be leading him. I was always an up-close person and I stood nearby and watched them. When Ray Charles died I had a great recollection of going back and seeing those times because the man came to Chestertown more than once. He practically lived here.

SYLVIA: There was something about the town that they really liked. Because in my young day when Patti Labelle and the Bluebells came to town, they would walk up the street liked they owned it .... walking in their curlers and their Capri shorts ...standing out there in the road.

ROSIE: I think Patti came here even when there wasn't a show. *(laughter)*

ROSIE: Mr. Graves' Uptown Club was the place to go! If a holiday came up and something wasn't happening at Charlie's, well, the town was dead. And the town is still dead today. The entertainment is gone.

SYLVIA: I thought I was everything when I got to go in there without getting permission. They used to have those matinees. I'd make sure I got my house cleaning done so I could be there and get a table. And I'd see all these people. They came from Delaware, and everywhere: good music, good food, and, sometimes, fights.

SYLVIA: I can remember when James Brown's bus came up Lynchburg Street, pulled up in front of our house, backed up and parked. Mom and her friends dressed up and went to Charlie's, and the last words out of their mouths were: "Now don't you come around that corner." Well...they just shouldn't have said it, because we needed to get our little peek. So we waited until she got in there good, and we went on in, and crawled in through the crowd on our hands and knees, got our peek and went back home.

ROSIE: The entertainers, before they got really big, were like ordinary people, and they associated with town-people like they always knew you. Remember when Little Richard came to town and needed a hairdo? He refused to go on stage without the hairdo. So Ms. Marion Lindsey did his hair... remember? She was a beautician on Lynchburg Street and he went there and got his hair done. Cause he's cute now, and he was cute back then.

And when James Brown started getting bigger and bigger, and more people were coming to see him from everywhere, so they took it down to the Armory.

I asked my mother a month in advance could I go see James Brown. She said no. Well "No" always meant "Yes" to me. I was like that then, and I'm like that now. I started getting my little clothes together. You HAD to have the new outfit. And it has to match. It was me and five more girls; we were all going to dress alike. I think it was black and white saddle shoes, socks that matched, black skirts....

SYLVIA: ...sharp!

ROSIE: I start buying my little stuff and leaving it at their house. And the night that James Brown comes I see my brothers getting ready. It was all right for them to go. I said, umm-humm, when they go to bed I'll sneak out and get dressed, so I snuck out, got dressed and went on down to James Brown. I did not care when I got home if I got beat, scorned or whatever. I was going! And my brothers came up to me and said, "What're you doing here? Mom is looking for you!" But I said to myself, I'm not going home 'til the last dance! It was a great time.

SYLVIA: I can remember when I was part of a local band. Charlie had his forty-some anniversary. Our band was Black Soul, and the girl singers were called the Blackettes. He had a great big table for his family and his brother came down from Jersey. And it was so special we went out and bought these green gowns with the back cut out. We sang our hearts out because we knew we were part of something special.

ROSIE: I would base this on the Apollo...it was a culture center. It was entertainment: you saw dancing, and every once in a while the locals thought they could sing and they wanted to get up there and show-case themselves. No matter how it looked to some people, that was all we had. You have to sit back and embrace it today, 'cause there was a lot coming out of there in the form of art. I can remember those line dances.

PEARL: The Madison.

ROSIE: Yes, and those dance contests they had. There were guys coming from Annapolis. They were all tall men and they could step! That was the entertainment. They would push the chairs back and they would have a Chestertown group on the side, another group and maybe a Philadelphia group.

SYLVIA: Back then it was hand-dancing time. I remember seeing couples swinging across the floor.

LESLIE: What were some of the other dances?

ROSIE: There was one called Kill that Roach....

PEARL: *(laughter)* I don't even remember that one.

[On June 1, 1988, in the wake of a concerted police raid and drug bust, a bulldozer demolition wiped out The Uptown Club in a matter of an hour.]

SYLVIA: It was heartbreaking, when it started going way down. And then they had that great big drug bust. They had all these people laying out on the floor. I was getting ready to go, because I wanted to get my last good-bye. But people were running up and saying don't go down there. And there were helicopters flying around, and I stood there and watched them knock the place down, it hurt me to my heart, it really did.

ROSIE: It took something out of our town, an era that was gone. The drug epidemic came in, and the place really went down.

PEARL: And Charlie was older then, too. And if he didn't let them in, that would be a problem.

ROSIE: They should have named something like a road after him. Charlie Graves' Way, or something.

LESLIE: What were some of the segregation issues at the time?

ROSIE: To know the closeness of the community that you live in is a beautiful thing. Compared to big-city living this is paradise. The only thing though, looking back, about Chestertown, that was sad to me, is I did not have... not one... white friend. To look back and understand the era that I lived in, that was devastating. To never know or never have any connection with someone my own age of another race. I didn't get that feeling until I moved to the city at the age of twenty-three and met white friends. And I thought Oh my! What a waste.

It was really a Jim Crow town... I won't say there was a lot of hatred then, but it was the way. By going away and coming back, I've picked up on some of it still here. And I can tell the ones who have been transplanted here. And as life goes on, layers go down, and soon it will stop. And with everyone commuting now, it's changing.... That can be good and it can be bad.... When you have families moving in from the cities, and different parts of the world, you bring in new changes. When I hear older folks talking and saying "I wish it was like it was" I know they were regular home people.

We were blessed to have Mr. Charlie Graves' Uptown Club in our time. The performers who are still on the circuit that we go see today, we say Oh My! And I can go anywhere and meet someone today who remembers Chestertown, someone who came to see a B.B. King concert or one of the performances.

Recently I met a man who couldn't believe that we had seen all these artists. Not in little Chestertown... you didn't expect that.... But it was the truth! This was the Apollo of the '50s. It was a time of change, and time of Black culture, and we saw all these artists. It's the truth! The local white people didn't come, but white people from the cities would drop down.... They were the die-hards, and they enjoyed it.

And it was a beautiful time.

Rupture

MEREDITH DAVIES HADAWAY

Together, in our small boat, we troll the waters
beneath Fossil Rock—a carved-out ledge that hangs
above the Chester's western bank and teems
with prehistoric sea-life frozen in the cliff.
Downriver, on the eastern edge, geologists
have discovered that a matching cliff preserves
the other half of creatures interrupted
in their journey into stone. A perfect

fit, if only these two halves could ever
reunite. We troll beneath the one
and then continue down the other side. Fish
are drawn to rocks as if they sense their history
and their future, both. We drag our baited line
through water, stop, rebait and start again.
How much farther, we wonder, in our lifetime,
will these two shorelines drift apart?

The Freedom Riders Come to Chestertown

SHEILA WEST AUSTRIAN

WASHINGTON COLLEGE, like the rest of Maryland's Eastern Shore in 1962, seemed almost untouched by the social forces ripping apart racial segregation in schools, restaurants and hotels across the nation. And before gentrification imposed today's economic segregation, the races lived in close and cordial proximity throughout Chestertown, with pockets of black families remaining in the historic district, especially down Cannon Street. College President Daniel Gibson worked hard to maintain good relations with the community, but Freedom Riders were scheduled to visit Chestertown and he was sure some of his students would join the expected civil rights demonstrations. That could cause problems with the town, but he strongly believed the college should not interfere with the students' right of free speech. Gibson was correct to worry, but Chestertown's social fabric ultimately was strong enough to cope with this new challenge.

Washington College was small, financially strapped with fewer than 500 students, and extremely homogenous. Of 145 new students in 1962, 79 were from Maryland and most of the rest from other Mid-Atlantic states. Gibson had convinced the Board to move toward an enrollment of 750, but the admissions yield rate remained disappointingly low, amid faculty fears that growth would merely buttress the school's reputation as a haven for the academically challenged.

Washington College certainly was a party school in the 1960s; issues of *The Elm* are filled with articles and photos depicting a whirl of dances and parties, many sponsored by the fraternities and sororities. The Kappa Alpha fraternity had hosted a Southern Ball the previous spring, with couples passing through an arch of swords raised by fraternity brothers dressed in pseudo-Confederate uniforms. An African-American band, the Pipe Dreamers, played "rhythmic music" at the Intrafraternity Council Dance in 1962, but no black guests appeared in the photo. Competition for the yearly Best-Dressed Girl contest was fierce. Robert Cleaver, who graduated in 1958, recalls no student discussions of integration issues but does remember an exhilarating Little Richard performance at the Uptown Club. He also remembers President Gibson placed the honky-tonk, a few steps from the campus, off limits when he learned students had "integrated" the black music club.

Students were concerned about broader issues as well. A test given at the college in March would give local draft boards "evidence of [which young men had] aptitude for continued undergraduate and graduate study." John Glenn had "conquered space" on February 20, and a Washington College graduate, Arthur Crisfield '59, was among the first Peace Corps volunteers sent to Thailand. Students may have been geographically isolated, but they also were part of the new generation inspired by President Kennedy.

Theoretically, the college was not a segregated institution, for the admissions policy did not explicitly exclude blacks. The Registrar at the time, Ermon Foster, later told history professor Nathan Smith that any applications from African-Americans had been rejected. By the late 1950s, however, the administration quietly enrolled a few African-American students. Thomas Morris, an all-round athlete and an academic achiever in the class of 1962, had been the first. Two black women, Pat Godbolt and Dale Patterson, also were on campus that year.

Their presence generated some of the tension between President Gibson and the Board. When integration was first discussed, one Board member had fretted about the extra expense to the college. Wouldn't it be very costly, he had pointed out, to build separate dorms, toilets and dining rooms? He was horrified to learn that the facilities would be shared. Another member of the Board vocally denounced integration as the "ruination" of the college. The college probably had felt daring when it decided to "experiment" with a few black students, but newly hired faculty were disappointed by the slow progress. Nathan Smith, recruited to Chestertown from Chicago, had asked for assurance that the college was not segregated before taking the position. He found the on-paper and on-the-ground situations quite different.

Neither Washington College nor Chestertown were comfortable places for black students in 1962. Dale Patterson, who grew up in strictly segregated Baltimore, recalls the 1960s as "the decade from hell." She enjoyed her chemistry classes, served as an RA, and worked in the dining hall to supplement scholarships and loans. Only fifteen years old when she matriculated, Patterson didn't have much of a social life, for the sororities wouldn't pledge blacks and she was too timid to venture into town. "I just decided that I would not ever go to the movie in Chestertown, because I refused to sit upstairs. I also did not want to be lynched." Although Patterson noted that the college curriculum included no facets of black culture, she did give black music credit for breaking down barriers. "To my ways of thinking," she said. "Berry Gordy single-handedly overcame the situation with Motown since everyone, black and white, wanted to hear the Supremes, the Temptations and the Miracles."

Chestertown itself remained deeply divided along racial lines. Most black residents worked as farm laborers or in food processing plants. Aside from the black Garnett School and the black churches, there were few middle-class jobs open to African Americans. At Washington College, blacks were employed as kitchen or maintenance workers. They appear in yearbooks, but only as nameless faces in group photographs.

Professor Smith and several other faculty members attended meetings of the new NAACP branch. The organization concentrated on improving conditions at the local hospital, which maintained segregated and inferior facilities for the black patients. Concerned white faculty wives, members of the American Association of University Women, had participated in a survey of the segregated slum housing adjacent to the campus. They found that many black homes had no indoor plumbing and that fires from kerosene heaters were common. AAUW activists also interviewed local school board members to determine why Chestertown public schools remained segregated, despite the 1954 Supreme Court decision and the fact that most of the Western Shore had begun full integration in 1955. A senior faculty member bragged to the women about the existing system used to prove Chestertown schools were not segregated. Any black student wanting to transfer had to apply to the Board of Education. The principal of Garnett School then would convince the student to stay at Garnett, which at that time contained grades one through twelve. Faculty who shared the local anti-integration ethos often asked their colleagues' wives, "Why aren't you in your kitchens? Why are you bothering about this stuff?"

For white citizens, Chestertown seemed almost like an idealized Norman Rockwell community. The *Kent County News*, a typical small town weekly, gave fulsome coverage to garden club meetings, golf tournaments, agricultural news and high school sports. The biggest event of the year was probably the introduction of dial telephones. No need to tell an operator the number, just listen for "a steady humming sound" and make the connection yourself. Kent County still had four high schools (in Galena and Rock Hall, as well as the two in Chestertown), a skating rink in Worton, and even illegal slot machines at the Kitty Knight House.

But until 1962, the town's black citizens were all but invisible in the public record. The paper rarely showed any black faces, and then almost always in the two columns dedicated to African-American affairs: one for Garnett School and the other the social "News from Butlertown." Where white teens listed a wide range of future aspirations, the Garnett School graduating elite were more likely to cite barber, beautician or stenographer as plans for the future. And where white newsmakers were normally named in the headline, African-Americans were not, as in a perfectly race-neutral article titled "County Negro Falls Off Boat; Is Drowned."

Most white residents probably considered themselves fair-minded and reasonable, for their lives rarely intersected with their black neighbors on issues of substance. That placid situation changed in February, when Freedom Riders crossed the Chesapeake Bay Bridge.

Freedom Riders, or busloads of white and black civil rights activists, had been making their non-violent demand for integrated access to public facilities in other states and cities for months. The Eastern Shore's relative isolation ended on the third of February, a cold and rainy Saturday, when "two big Greyhound buses" and "nine or ten carloads of persons" arrived at the Bethel A.M.E. Church in Chestertown. Several dozen police cars, most from other jurisdictions, were waiting for them. So were hundreds of bystanders and about eighty cars at Bud Hubbard's, a restaurant with a racist reputation now filled with angry white men drinking beer.

A little after three in the afternoon, crowds near Bud's started pummeling the picketers, who eventually fled back to the church. Later "an angry mob of fifty Chestertown Negroes" returned to Bud's, where police managed to avert a real brawl. According to *Elm* reporter Walt Marschner, several Washington College students marched with the picketers or met with the demonstrators at Bethel. He described an evening rally at the church that was "packed with emotion," where tired demonstrators sang civil rights songs and danced in an impromptu conga line. College students, a few professors, and concerned black Chestertown residents, perhaps for the first time together, earnestly discussed efforts to solve the town's racial problems. The reporter learned that the Garnett School principal, previously one of the most respected men in the black community, had left town rather than meet with the Freedom Riders. By standing with the white establishment, he lost much of his authority.

The *Elm* provided excellent news coverage of the Freedom Ride, with good background information and hour-by-hour commentary. The article was so good, in fact, that a Washington College professor with Supreme Court contacts sent each justice a copy. But the *Elm*'s editor in chief, whom Marschner characterized as an "Eastern Shore segregationist," put his own stamp on the event with the misleading headline, "Freedom Raids Plague Chestertown."

The *Kent County News* also played the story on its first page, focusing on the few arrests and giving the fracas at Bud's special notice. In an editorial, "The Point Has Been Made," the paper charged that the "so-called" Freedom Rides were merely a publicity ploy. Local restaurants, it asserted, had the legal right to "cater to any clientele they may choose." A letter to the editor, from a Kennedyville resident, contained unintentional humor with a non-standard version of an old saying. Complaining about Negro demands, the writer warned, "Give them the finger and they will demand the whole hand."

The *News* also printed letters from local African Americans who supported integration. One Garnett School graduate told readers about taking her family to the drug store for ice cream. "I don't suppose you can imagine," she wrote, "just how to go about explaining to small children why they can spend their money in such places, but the privilege of sitting down and eating is out of the question." A few months later, the *News* ran a positive article about "Project Eastern Shore," an interracial effort to improve community relations through a series of lectures and discussions. Whereas serious and violent protests continued for several years in nearby Cambridge, Chestertown's leadership seems to have accepted the inevitability of social change and worked to make it happen peacefully.

President Gibson consulted with the Chairman of the Board of Visitors and Governors and then issued a statement four days after the demonstrations. Gibson chose his words carefully, to offend as few as possible. He left Washington College solidly on the fence, advising:

Washington College considers participation in activities supporting integration a matter to be decided by the individual students and their parents. The College neither encourages nor prohibits participation in sit-ins, petitions, etc. The College, however, does not condone violations of the law.

The *Elm's* editor, H. Allen Stafford, continued to ridicule civil rights activism in bold type responses to student letters in favor of integration. He described the typical Freedom Rider as "a juvenile delinquent who enters uninvited, inflicts wounds, leaves, and only the wound remains." Pitting community mores against "youthful exhibitionism," Stafford preached that "long-range interests" were harmed by demonstrations. Even the relatively liberal President Gibson, with typical Eastern Shore disregard for haste, thought integration might come to Washington College "in one hundred years.... In any case, no sooner than fifty years."

During the few weeks that demonstrations took place in Chestertown, President Gibson downplayed any college activism to members of the Board. In a March 19 agenda sent in advance of a regular meeting on March 24, Gibson said "small numbers of students" and, to the best of his knowledge, "no faculty" had demonstrated. When a student handbill urged participation, the President convinced the author of the impropriety of invoking the college name or using college mail facilities. He warned the Board that while "some ill will in the local community" resulted from the student action, banning participation would have worse consequences, including a "strong reaction within the faculty itself." And, as he reminded, "the vast majority of our students are not participating or even sympathetic to the methods being used."

After a few weeks, the organized protestors moved on to different locales. Most Washington College students resumed the normal routine of classes, sports and social events. The guys at Bud's kept drinking beer and talking tough but the town quietly moved to integrate its commercial and public facilities. Stam's and the Chestertown Pharmacy just removed the stools from the soda fountain. By 1963, the movie theater, bowling alley and skating rink had dropped official segregation. The public schools and hospital followed suit. Washington College enrolled more black students during the next three decades but, until the school made real efforts to increase diversity in the 1990s, few African Americans even considered applying.

Even today, African American college applicants probably think carefully before deciding to attend Washington College. In 2005 there were about fifty African American students and only a handful of black faculty. The local black middle-class remains miniscule and voluntary social and economic segregation usually keeps the races apart.

Chestertown's African American citizens generally do not attend college lectures, worship at the "white" churches, join the country club, or eat at table-service restaurants. Urban renewal housing units have replaced the slums around Bethel Church, but unemployed young black men still slouch at the corner of High Street and College Avenue. They may have even less in common with today's Washington College students than the two groups did in 1962. At least then, the dream was new and more than legal equality seemed possible.

Swish Nicholson: Local Hero and Baseball Great

JACK GILDEN

It was back in the day when a greasy old filling station on Route 213 was kind of like Chestertown's Ellis Island. There was a Trailways stop there that offered a couple of visitors every day their entrance into the ancient place. That's where I disembarked and walked into the town for the first time in my life. I was eighteen.

As I strolled around the place before a scheduled admissions appointment at Washington College, I was oblivious to the incredible 18th-century federal architecture. And the languid pace and rhythms of the town, a source of charm to so many others, only struck me as evidence of insignificance. When I failed to find any statues, plaques or notations of historical residents or events, I concluded that it was a 300-year-old chronic condition. This complete lack of bustle or civic ambition suited me, since I expected to spend the next four years here engaged in serious study. (The serious study of brunettes, blondes and redheads.)

All of this notwithstanding, I consciously decided to live in Chestertown the summer between my junior and senior years. I stayed for two reasons: First, I had to make up a math course that I had failed, even though the thing was so easy it was probably invented to keep the Upstate dumb-dumbs eligible for varsity lacrosse. Second, I was avoiding going back home at a particularly difficult time in our family life—the lawn-cutting season at my father's house.

In addition to my "studies," I took a job in the office of college relations writing press releases and other materials relating to our membership in the Mid-Atlantic Conference. It should have been a mostly forgettable experience except that in my zeal to spice up our prose for a league publication I referred to several rivals as "pansies." This description skulked past both my bosses and the editors at the conference office, but seemed to wiggle and gyrate lasciviously under the outraged noses of the insulted schools' pedagogues.

Instantly, the offended parties struck back with censure and epithets aimed at both Washington College and me. The school, seeing its reputation sink with every single word I pecked out on its behalf, decided it was time to give me a new assignment. I was taken off public relations and told instead to write a feature story for the college magazine about Bill "Swish" Nicholson, the best athlete in school history. The assignment, I was told, should last the rest of the summer. That wasn't an estimate of time, but a rather forceful demand.

I approached the project with mild interest. Swish Nicholson was an old outfielder who prowled the verdant lawns of the National League in the era of Ted Williams and Joe DiMaggio. I was a lover of baseball and an enthusiastic reader of its history since a boyhood spent worshipping Brooks Robinson. My obsession with the game grew as I did, so that by the time I entered high school my father wondered out loud how I was failing "Introduction to Typing" (among other classes) and yet somehow knew the current batting averages of every utility infielder on the Yankees and Red Sox (two teams I detested). "When I was in school," he thundered, "the kids went outside during typing class and smoked dope. And they still got a 'C'!"

Despite my interest in baseball I had never even heard of Swish. Therefore my 20-year-old brain instantly dismissed him as a "Chestertown celebrity," a big leaguer, maybe, but long forgotten. In 1986 he was nothing more than an aging farmer and a hunter, isolated and obscure. If he was a big fish it was only in relation to the puny guppies plopping around the Chester puddle.

In the 1940s, the Eastern Shore produced two National League sluggers, Bill "Swish" Nicholson (at left) and Jimmy Foxx of Sudlersville.

Even the shoddy research of which I was capable quickly revealed that I was a moron. (Why was I the last to know?) Swish Nicholson was a big star in his day, as big as the National League had to offer. Spending almost his entire career with the Chicago Cubs and the Philadelphia Phillies, he played a pivotal role in two historic pennant races. In 1945 he helped the Cubs achieve their last World Series appearance in the 20th century. And in 1950 he was one of Philadelphia's famous "Whiz Kids," a group of upstarts that unexpectedly grabbed the pennant.

Nicholson's individual accomplishments were more than impressive. He led the National League in home runs and runs batted in (rbi's) in 1943, and then again in 1944, achieving two-thirds of a Triple Crown in two straight years. Of all the great and fearsome sluggers to ever play the game, very few had ever accomplished this.

On July 23, 1944, facing the New York Giants, he bashed his fourth consecutive home run. When he came up with a chance to make it five in a row, the bases were loaded. Giants manager, Mel Ott, had seen enough. He simply surrendered and ordered his pitcher to intentionally walk Nicholson. Giving a player the free pass with the bases loaded is one of the rarest occurrences in baseball. Though there is some dispute about this, it is believed Nicholson was just the third batter in history to be accorded this extreme show of respect. It wouldn't happen again for another fifty-four years, when Arizona waved the white flag at Barry Bonds, who may or may not have been enjoying a better career through chemistry.

In 1944 Nicholson was just one vote behind Marty Marion of the St. Louis Cardinals for the National League Most Valuable Player award.

By the time I arrived at Nicholson's farm, I had completed my background research. Viewing photos in an old school file of both the man and the ballplayer, it was hard to ignore that he was a pretty nice-looking guy in his prime—tall, solidly built and thick of hair. When he smiled he was all flashing teeth and dimples. In those days of elaborate haberdashery, he sported crisp suits, snappy fedoras and wingtips shined to a glassy perfection. He didn't look so much like a baseball hero as he did a Hollywood director's conception of one.

And it was a good thing that he looked like a hero. After his two historic seasons in 1943 and '44, his career seriously declined. He went from leading the league with thirty-three homers to managing just thirteen in 1945. The next season, at the prime age of thirty-two, he would hit only eight. This was a mystery I intended to explore with him.

Nicholson's farm sat along the Langford Creek. His home was simple but attractive. The front porch featured a couple of old hunting dogs, drowsing in the early evening. As I approached the house these brutes lifted their heads indolently, pushed up on their paws and wagged their forlorn tails.

I rapped on the screen door a couple of times and Swish appeared. He was no longer a 205-pound ballplayer. He was seventy-three, trim but sinewy, and probably still a pretty tough customer. The thick, perfect brown hair I saw in his playing-day photos was gone, all gone; he was bald. I myself had an exceedingly beautiful head of brown hair at that time, and I remember thinking: "If it could happen to him…." But I stopped myself since the notion was preposterous, paranoid and, if possible, too tragic to contemplate. Swish extended his hand to shake and welcomed me into his home. We sat down in his living room, and after exchanging stiff pleasantries I commenced the interview. My first question was calculated to be easy. "How did you get the name Swish?"

"Well, I had a habit," he said. "I would slowly swing my bat across the plate while I was waiting for the pitcher to deliver. I was a pretty big fella and I swung a pretty big stick, so in Brooklyn they started chanting, "swissshhh" every time I swung the bat. Eventually everybody called me that."

As we talked baseball the many obstacles of formality, familiarity and age faded until we were just two guys discussing a game we both loved. Eventually the conversation took on a warmth I hadn't expected, and he started volunteering stories that weren't even on my list. In one of them Nicholson plays a key role in a tale that later became celebrated in American literature and film.

"I played ball with a first baseman named Eddie Waitkus," he said. "We were roommates. One day I was in the hotel and Eddie was out when a call came from a girl. She said her name was Burns and that she had grown up with Eddie in Boston. She was staying in our hotel and said that she would like him to stop by so they could catch up. When I gave him the message, he said that he didn't remember her but that the name sounded familiar since it was Irish and typical of the Boston area. He called her back and went up to see her. When he entered her room she had a gun and shot him. She had been following him around. I guess she was in love with him. But they had never met."

That awful event became the basis for Bernard Malamud's *The Natural*, a dark novel about an extraordinarily gifted ballplayer who, in a moment of moral repose, is shot by a beautiful stranger and robbed of his grand potential. In the early 1980s this story was memorably adapted for film by Barry Levinson, starring Robert Redford.

There were mysteries to Nicholson, too. When I asked him why his skills diminished in the prime of his career, he candidly confessed a great fear. "In 1945 I should have had my best season. The Cubs won the pennant and I was going to the World Series. But I wasn't myself. Something was working on me."

Nicholson didn't know what that something was, but he had an idea. He was losing strength and feeling generally unwell and his imagination was running away with him. He had convinced himself that he was being ravaged by cancer. Fearing a confirmation of his blackest thoughts, he suffered in silence and resisted medical intervention. Finally, and probably at the insistence of the ball club, he was examined, but misdiagnosed. "Nothing wrong but that you smoke and drink too much," the doctor told him. Nicholson said that it wasn't true, but he let the matter drop.

After a lackluster performance in the World Series, the one in which the Cubs were supposedly cursed by an irate farmer and a billy goat, his career sputtered for several more seasons, reviving then dropping. By 1949 his best days were behind him and so were the Cubs. The former star attraction was unceremoniously traded to Philadelphia.

The Phillies were assembling enough good young talent to seriously contend for the National League flag. Nicholson could have provided valuable veteran leadership to a club like that, but he could barely contribute. He was feeling worse and worse, and losing weight at an alarming rate. Finally on Labor Day, one of the baseball season's many benchmarks, he collapsed. *The Sporting News* called it "a near fatal attack."

In our conversation Nicholson disputed the severity of his condition, but admitted that he was taken to the hospital where he was finally diagnosed properly. The ailment that robbed him of so many potentially great seasons was not cancer; it was diabetes. "A few people in my mother's family had it," he said. "Why didn't I think of it?"

After concluding business we ambled toward the front door laughing and chatting. On a table near the door, he had prepared a treat for me. Artifacts of his big league career were laid out on the surface for me to examine. He let me hold these great and dated tools of his first career. It occurred to me while I gripped one of his old Louisville Sluggers, an instrument far too big for me, that I must have appeared like a little boy. Nicholson's mood changed, he became very serious and started to tell me the story of how he had lost one of his two sons. "He came here very late one night and asked me for some money," he said. "When I wouldn't give it to him he took off for Florida, hitchhiking. He got hit by a truck on the way down there."

I got the impression that his son had been lost to him some time before then. I only managed to say, "I'm sorry to hear that."

"You know, I don't tell very many people about that," he said. "Please come back here anytime you like."

The next time I saw Swish, about a month later, was not at his home, but at the Kent & Queen Anne's Hospital. He was laid up. Word of my story had gotten around the Eastern Shore, and several newspapers sought my permission to republish it. One of them, the *Easton Star Democrat*, made it the cover article for its weekly magazine, *Currents*. When I walked into Swish's hospital room, I had a few copies fresh off the press under my arm.

Nicholson wasn't feeling well, but he was extremely pleased to see me. He introduced me to his roommate, another elderly man who was an old friend of his. I showed them the magazine and they sat up in their beds while I read. I looked up occasionally to see their bristling gray cheeks and their rapt attention. My piece was essentially a defense of Bill Nicholson's career. It was about a man who started with incredible talent and who ascended to the highest heights in his profession. It explained the mystery of his sudden demise on his terms, with complete sympathy for his point of view. When I finished reading, neither man spoke for a while. I looked at Nicholson and I could plainly see him awash in the pleasure of it. He commented on my writing style, which in a stream-of-consciousness sort of way led the two old men to spew some outrageous epithets about a newspaperman they both knew and despised. Gathering himself together before I left, Nicholson cheerfully told me: "You should become a professional writer." I said thanks, but after listening to those two work over the profession I had no idea if it was a compliment.

Ultimately the piece was published in the college alumni publication, reprinted in two Eastern Shore newspapers, and sought by two different national sports magazines—*Baseball Digest* and a startup called *Sports Heritage*. I sold it to the latter publication for the princely sum of $500, and then promptly blew it all on a preposterous 1978 Chrysler Cordoba. The signature feature of that old rust box was a roof of raw steel. According to the guy who sold me the car, the vinyl had been peeled away by a committee of monkeys at a New Jersey wildlife preserve. And who would make that up?

In the process of enlarging the story for *Sports Heritage* I tried to contact a few of Nicholson's former teammates. The only one I reached was the most famous of them, Richie Ashburn. I tracked him down on the road where he was working as a broadcast announcer for his old team, the Philadelphia Phillies. Ashburn had been a centerfielder in the golden era of that position, in the years of Mickey Mantle, Willie Mays and Duke Snyder. Though not as well known as that trio of star New Yorkers, Ashburn was a career .308 batter who set several major league records with his glove. At the time of our conversation he was a few years short of being elected to the Hall of Fame. Ashburn played side-by-side with Nicholson, a right fielder, so I asked him how well Swish handled his glove. Assuming that Nicholson was competent though unspectacular, I compared him to Gary Roenicke, a Baltimore player of my era. Ashburn quickly rebuked me: "Nicholson was an outstanding fielder. He wasn't at all average like the player you mentioned." Then he asked me a question: "Why are you calling to ask about Bill? He's ok, isn't he?"

The desperation that was implicit in the question was sad in its own way. No one would have feared a reporter inquiring about the career of Williams or DiMaggio. Or even Ashburn. Because I was calling to ask about a long-forgotten player, because I was calling about Bill Nicholson, Richie Ashburn assumed I was preparing an obituary.

In fact, with a little perspective, I came to realize that the opposite was true. Instead of sculpting his death mask, I was affording him new real estate in the sun, a chance to have his sultry days reexamined and contextualized for contemporary consideration.

And, indeed, he experienced one last revival. With a surge of interest in his career by the town and his friends, a testimonial dinner was held for him at Washington College. The proceeds were used to erect a handsome statue of him in Chestertown. I attended that dinner and when I arrived, I immediately sought him out to say hello. But I was taken aback by his appearance. He was thin and enfeebled, no longer himself, but he was happy to see me and we exchanged pleasantries. Several former major league players and coaches attended this evening of a thousand corny stories. The best one, the only one I remember, was from an old teammate who recalled a long-ago plane trip with Swish and the team. "We were bouncing around and we were afraid the plane was going to go down. So we turned to Bill—he was our leader and a real veteran—and we said, 'Bill, do something.' Well, he calmly removed his hat and passed it around and instructed all of the players to put money in it. Finally, one of us had the courage to ask him what in the hell he was doing. 'We're all gonna die,' he said, 'so I figured we ought do something religious.'"

With yet another baseball season in motion, I recently dug out my old article about Swish Nicholson and reread it. I was shocked at how mawkish and poorly written I found it. I was embarrassed to see it. In retrospect, all the undue credit I received for it made me something of a "Chestertown celebrity," the sneering sobriquet I had imagined for Nicholson himself before I met him.

When I wrote my first piece about Nicholson in 1986, I was precisely the same age he was when he began his baseball career. As I write these words, I am the same age he was when he quit the game. Much is made of how ballplayers "retire" while they are still young, but I think the best of them hang it up not in their youth, but rather in the first flickering, almost imperceptible, days of old age. I'm married now and the father of two. My own career has flashed great promise and suffered humiliating and inexplicable defeats. I have returned to Chestertown many times since I was graduated from Washington College in 1987. One of those trips was to attend Swish's funeral, which was held in a rustic church just a mile or two down the road from his farm. When I go back to Chestertown these days, I always stop downtown to look at him in bronze. If a visitor came today and wandered around, like I did so many years ago, he would finally have a plaque to read. But thinking it over I would say the Chestertown to which I first came was a far better place; because in those days, Bill Nicholson really lived there.

Chester River Sketches with Apologies to Bashō

PAT HEROLD NIELSEN

VISION
It's moonless when we graze the pound net—
Our eyes too old for this black night.

HOT AIR
In the cabin, the boys nap with mosquitoes
While we search for the breeze.

GOOD LUCK
The day the tiller breaks the anchor chain goes too—
We drift and sip beer.

CHESTER RIVER LEGEND
Tallulah Bankhead is buried on Cacaway Island—
Google this.

PENNY SAVER
This old boat served us well—
Bowl food and bread, sunset and stars for dessert.

STRATEGIC PLANNING
Fluorescent light makes my head hurt—
Let's build a bonfire and tell stories.

In Pursuit of Revenue: Diary of the Schooner *Sultana*

KEES DE MOOY

Editor's Note: In the months when community volunteers in Chestertown were building an historically accurate replica of the 18th-century American-built schooner Sultana, *Kees de Mooy became intrigued with the history of the original. He began his investigation by transcribing the ship's logs, and then, with a grant from the Douglass Cater Society of Junior Fellows, visited all the ports the* Sultana *had seen, on American shores and in England. His senior thesis, on which this article is based, documents the exploits the* Sultana *made "in pursuit of revenue" for Mother Britain.*

IN THE MID-1760s, a crisis was developing between Britain and her American colonies. After more than 100 years of relative autonomy, Americans suddenly faced taxes imposed on them by British Parliament. British army and naval forces had defended the thirteen colonies in the French and Indian War, and tax revenues were needed to make up for the tremendous debts incurred during seven years of fighting.

In order to bring money into the Treasury, the Royal Navy was charged with aiding in the implementation of the Navigation Acts, which consisted of duties on many goods imported into the colonies. American merchants balked at what they considered to be unfair taxes, and circumvented customs ships by smuggling goods in all manner of small coasting vessels. In 1764, the British Admiralty purchased six American-built schooners to patrol the shallow waters preferred by smugglers. With thousands of miles of Atlantic coastline to guard, more vessels were needed and, four years later, a schooner built at the Boston shipyard of Benjamin Hallowell was sailed to England, where it was purchased and refitted for service on the North American Station.

This is the story of His Majesty's Armed Schooner *Sultana*, as told through logbook entries that begin in London's Deptford Dock, one of the largest naval yards in England.

July 18, 1768. Lying in Deptford Dock. Moderate & Fair Weather. People employed getting the Iron Ballast on board the Schooner.

On July 15, Captain John Inglis, an American-born Lieutenant in the Royal Navy, began the work of readying the *Sultana* for its mission in the colonies. As his crew of twenty-four men arrived over the course of several weeks, he had them install and rig new sails, build a brick ship stove and caulk the deck. Provisions including barrels of Irish sea bass, fresh beef, salted tongue, peas, bread, cheese, raisins and vinegar were stored in the hold. Casks of beer and brandy, the standard drink of sailors, were likewise stowed away. Eight one-half pound swivel guns were mounted on the sides of the schooner, and muskets, pistols and powder were brought below. On September 1, 1768, the *Sultana* steered out of the Thames and sailed westward across the Atlantic.

November 16, 1768. Moored in Boston harbor, the Long Wharf WSW one Cable's length. First part Moderate & Cloudy with Rain. Middle & Later parts Strong Gales & Cloudy. At 7 AM Manned Ship for General Gage Going on board of the Romney as did all the Ships of the Fleet. The Boats Employed in Landing the Troops out of the Transports.

After a rough trans-Atlantic crossing lasting several harrowing weeks, during which the schooner nearly capsized, Captain Inglis and his men sailed into Boston Harbor, where a tense standoff was brewing. Several months prior to their arrival, local customs officials had seized John Hancock's sloop *Liberty* on suspicion of smuggling, and fierce riots erupted in the city. In a move that was guaranteed to provoke further confrontations, British officials decided to send two regiments of troops to occupy the city, and two additional regiments were sent from Ireland. Arriving shortly after the *Sultana*, the troops were ferried to shore with cutters belonging to the schooner and other Royal Navy ships anchored in Boston Harbor. Treated as foreign occupiers, the soldiers frequently clashed with Bostonians, culminating in the Boston Massacre of March 1770.

December 25, 1768. Newport Harbor. Moderate & Clear. Seized the Royal Charlotte Brig with 6 Cases of Gin. At 1/2 past went on board the Brig & Found the Customhouse officer on Shore. Seized the Brig with all her tackling & Left an officer on board with 3 men & nailed up her hatches for the Benefit of his Majesty & heirs.

From Boston, Captain Inglis was ordered to sail to Rhode Island, a hotbed of smugglers. One week after anchoring near Newport, Captain Inglis spotted a brig, the *Royal Charlotte*, surreptitiously unloading cargo near shore. Discovering that the crates contained contraband gin, Inglis had the ship seized according to maritime law. One day earlier, Newport Customhouse officials had boarded the same brig and had placed one of their men on board, but he was bribed and sent ashore. The Newport Customhouse and the *Sultana* filed competing claims against the *Royal Charlotte*, drawing out the legal proceedings to the point that neither party stood to profit. The ship was returned to its owners after two months of legal wrangling, during which only the gin was condemned.

April 1, 1769. Moored in Rhode Island Harbor. Fresh breezes. Received from the Senegal half a Cord of wood. Broke one of the boat oars by Accident. Prince Gould, a black man entered on board.

Keeping his schooner manned was a constant challenge for Inglis and other officers in the British Navy. Low pay, cramped quarters and dangerous working conditions caused sailors to run away at a very high rate. To ensure that ships maintained an adequate complement of men, press gangs frequently roamed the streets and drinking establishments of seaside towns. Volunteers were also essential. Prince Gould, a 45-year-old free black man, volunteered to serve following the escape of several crewmen. When Gould came on board, he was examined and discovered to have a herniated abdomen, likely the result of strenuous lifting, a constant shipboard activity. The combination of advanced age (most sailors were in their teens and twenties) and medical disability limited his effectiveness, but he served ably for eight months before being discharged in Virginia.

October 7, 1769. Moored in Hampton Road, Virginia. Strong breezes and Cloudy. Sent the boats to search two Vessels within the Capes. Boarded a brig from Leith with coal bound to Norfolk. Sent the Cutter to Hampton for sweet water & in coming off she was overset & the said water was lost & no part of them could be saved, being some time before the people were discovered hanging to the boat.

From September 1769 to August 1770, *Sultana* was stationed near the mouth of Chesapeake Bay. The region was widely regarded as one of the most commercially advantageous areas in the world, and thus drew many settlers to its shores. By 1770, more than 750,000 people had flocked there to take advantage of its fertile lands and well-stocked waters. Smuggling was prevalent, and the *Sultana* stopped and searched nearly 150 vessels in the area, during weather conditions that could turn dangerous very quickly. Headed back to the schooner from shore with fresh drinking water, the schooner's cutter capsized in rough waters, nearly drowning several men.

July 13, 1770. Smith Point SW 3 Leagues. Light breezes and cloudy. At 2 PM set the topsails, at 10 PM came to Anchor with the small bower in 9 fathoms water. Going down to Potomac River in company with the Boston.

Accompanied by H.M.S. *Boston*, *Sultana* sailed up the Potomac and anchored near Belvoir, the estate of George William Fairfax. Next door was Mount Vernon, the home of Fairfax's friend, George Washington, at that time a powerful member of the Virginia House of Burgesses. On July 29, Washington invited Captain Inglis and his pilot, David Bruce, to dinner. Washington corresponded with John Inglis's brother, Samuel, a prominent Norfolk merchant who was in partnership with Robert Morris, the future financier of the American Revolution. The subject of their conversation was not recorded. The *Sultana* sailed back to its station in Hampton Road after two weeks in the Potomac.

November 23, 1770. Fishers Island ENE 4 miles. Cloudy & Hazy thick weather. At 11 AM Boarded the Polly *Sloop Bound to Dartmouth with Ballast & Some Provisions & the Greyhound Sloop with wood to Nantucket Island. At 2 PM aired the sails. The people Employed Looking out for the two Sloop which were to Come From Amsterdam with Contraband Goods.*

Admiral Gambier, commander of the Royal Navy in North America, learned in early November that a shipment of illicit Dutch tea was headed to New York. Dutch tea, untaxed and cheaper than British tea, was smuggled into the colonies in large quantities. Gambier ordered Captain Inglis to block the northern approach to New York by cruising between Fishers Island and Montauk Point on Long Island. For two weeks the *Sultana* sailed back and forth, stopping and searching a variety of vessels. However, the smugglers evaded the blockade and safely offloaded their cargo in New York. Furious at the ease with which his blockade was eluded, Gambier appealed to the British Admiralty for additional patrol vessels, but his request was denied.

February 27, 1771. Newport Town, Rhode Island, NE by E 2 miles. First Part Fresh Gales & Thick Weather. Later part Squally with Rain & Snow. At 8 PM Let Go the Best Bower anchor For Fear of being Drove out to Sea by the Ice. Went 2 Cables Lengths Farther into the Cove & Came to anchor.

The winter of 1771 was particularly rough on the *Sultana* and her crew. Forced below deck during weeks of bitterly cold weather, the crew spent their days huddled around the relative warmth of the ship stove, performing menial tasks like repairing sails and ropes. However, even in sub-freezing temperatures, the men had to come on deck in shifts to break up the ice that formed around the schooner. Ice floes were a serious hazard to contend with, and the men had to shift anchorage often so that the boat would not be swept out to sea. Heavy snows meant frequent shoveling to keep the deck clear and to prevent melt water from leaking into the hold. Despite the crew's efforts, melting snow soaked everything below deck, making life miserable for everyone on board.

April 12, 1771. Anchored in Newport Harbor. Hard gales & Cloudy Weather. At 4 PM Manned and armed the Boat to go on Shore to Assist the Collector of His Majesty's Customs at Rhode Island. He Seized a Brig that was running their Cargo, & the Mob gathered & beat him, & threatened to pull down the Custom house & Seize on the King's property.

In the week prior to the *Sultana's* arrival, a Newport customs official had unsuccessfully attempted to seize the brig *Polly*, which was carrying contraband goods. Knocked unconscious and dragged into town by a mob, the customs official barely escaped with his life. The attackers returned and emptied out the suspected ship, then tarred and feathered a suspected informant. When the *Sultana* appeared several days later to transport a chest of customs revenues to Boston, the mob reassembled and threatened to destroy the Newport Customhouse. Captain Inglis responded to the crisis by sending fourteen heavily armed men to shore in the cutter. A tense standoff ensued, but the crowd was eventually dispersed without incident. Two days later, the money was taken on board *Sultana* and delivered to the Custom Commissioner in Boston.

September 10, 1771. Anchored off New Castle on Delaware. Light breezes with Cloudy & rain. At 4 PM Read the Articles of War to the Schooner's

Company. Punished Henry Black & Robert Whaley with 2 dozen lashes each for absenting themselves from their duty & attempting to run away.

The *Articles of War* was a set of navy regulations that governed behavior on board all Royal Navy vessels, and stipulated penalties for thirty-six shipboard offenses. Sailors charged with cursing, drunkenness, dereliction of duty, sleeping while on watch, disobeying an order, desertion or mutiny were liable to be punished with anywhere from twelve to one hundred lashes, or death in extreme cases. Sailors Henry Black and Robert Whaley ran away from the *Sultana's* cutter when it was sent ashore for supplies. They were apprehended by local authorities and put in jail, where they were picked up the following morning. Led back to the schooner in chains, the two men were tied to the mainmast with their arms over their heads and whipped with twenty-four blows of a cat o' nine tails in front of the entire crew. Eight months later, Henry Black fell and drowned while boarding a ship that had been stopped in the Delaware River. Four months after Black's death, Robert Whaley made his successful escape while *Sultana* was anchored near Philadelphia.

May 8, 1772. Delaware River. Strong Gales and Squally. Going down the River in pursuit of the Brig that brought in Prohibited Wine. In Company with the King George Customhouse boat. Boarded the Said Brig, and found on board her some empty wine & brandy Casks. Seized her on Suspicion.

Acting on a tip, the *Sultana* crew pursued and seized the brig *Carolina* on suspicion of smuggling. Captain Inglis placed his midshipman and six sailors on the prize and began to escort the vessel to the Philadelphia Customhouse. A menacing crowd formed on shore and, fearing an attack like one that had led to the near destruction of the local customs boat, *King George*, several months earlier, Inglis ordered his gunner to load six swivel cannon with grape shot. Fortunately, tide and wind cooperated to keep the *Sultana* and *Carolina* out of harm's way. Another Royal Navy ship arrived on the scene and helped to get the brig safely to

Philadelphia. One month later, the *Sultana's* crew was paid prize money stemming from the condemnation of the *Carolina*, the only recorded bounty that the men received during more than four years of service.

October 23, 1772. Cape Race NNE by E 49 Leagues. Hard Gales & Squally with rain. A great deal of Sea from the WSW board. At 2 PM Shipped a Sea. Filled the boat. Washed away the Companion & overset the binnacle. Laid the Schooner on her beam ends. Cut away the boat and let her go overboard to save the schooner. She righted.

In mid-October 1772, after fifty-four months of service on the coast of North America, Captain Inglis was ordered to sail the *Sultana* back to England. Admiral Montagu stated that the schooner was "too small and not able to encounter the heavy Gales of wind, especially in the Winter Season." One week into the trans-Atlantic journey, heavy swells engulfed the *Sultana*, nearly capsizing the vessel. The cutter was thrown into the sea and, sinking, pulled the schooner over even further. A quick-thinking crewman cut away the boat, allowing the schooner to right itself and thereby saving the lives of all on board. Heavy winds and rain followed the schooner all the way back to England.

December 7, 1772. Moored in Portsmouth Harbor. Moderate and hazy with drifting rain. Paid the Schooner's Company their wages.

Sultana finally arrived on the coast of England after an exhausting, rain-soaked six-week voyage. During a one-week delay before the schooner could dock in Portsmouth shipyard, storm seas broke over the deck and filled the hold. At last the schooner was escorted into the shipyard, where it was completely stripped of sails, rigging and supplies. On December 7, Captain Inglis made the last entry in his logbook. The men were paid off and most of them transferred to other ships in the harbor. After serving nearly five years in the colonies, Captain Inglis left the Royal Navy and traveled to Scotland for a needed vacation. On August 11, 1773, the *Sultana* was sold at auction to John Hook Jr. for

£85, less than one-third of the original purchase price. The eventual fate of the schooner is unknown, but it most likely spent the next few years along the coast of England as a trading vessel before succumbing to damage sustained in the American colonies. Inglis returned to service in the Royal Navy, rising eventually to the rank of Vice Admiral.

Breed: The Red Jellyfish

SARAH BLACKMAN

Under the docks—tea tureens of swamp water, the little snails clotting
    along eel grass—
my mother screes for red jellyfish. A jelly one the same pellucid color as
    my jelly

slipper—bought over protest, strap snapped in a week. Here is the wide
    green Bay, the buff
boat we will ride it. Further, past the gun tower and dim summer
    partridge, the chopped

fissures of water pressing water's back. Somehow, men have anchored a raft
so it both floats and tugs against its floating. Somehow, below the docks

the jellyfish pulse the same sudden thunder as cloud swells bursting
the crowded waterline. Osprey learns to call like a torn cat. In the middle

of the shell road, a matterhorn rises in perfect spirals—too slick to climb
we huddle together, exposed and infinite,
                runners on the hedgerow, pea vines tipped to bursting pods.

The Great Fire of 1916

WILLIAM L. THOMPSON

A LIGHT SNOW was falling upon the already whitened ground in the early morning hours of Sunday morning, January 16, 1916, when James Lecates—the watchman of the Pennsylvania Railroad yard—spied an orange glow in the direction of Washington College. Sensing calamity, Lecates sounded an engine whistle that tore the silence over sleeping Chestertown.

About the same time, William J. Wallace, president of the college sophomore class, was awake in his Middle Hall room helping a sick roommate when, looking out a window, he saw flames leaping from the rear side of the northern wing of William Smith Hall.

Wallace's shouts woke everyone in Middle Hall and other students quickly roused classmates and professors living in East and West halls. Within half an hour a crowd of students and townspeople—alerted by the locomotive whistle and the subsequent ringing of church bells—had gathered around Smith Hall. Flames, which apparently had originated in the janitor's basement utility room, spread throughout the structure so quickly that by the time the volunteer fire company reached campus, Smith Hall was nearly fully enveloped.

Some students tried connecting the fire hoses in Middle, East and West halls in order to direct water onto the blaze, but they were unable to coax anything from the pipes. Dragging the hose to the town water lugs at the foot of the campus, students were dismayed to discover that the fittings were not compatible.

Meanwhile, college president James W. Cain and a few students attempted to enter the building by the front steps. The heat foiled that attempt. At the rear of the building, Dr. J.S.W. Jones and student Donald Tydings succeeded in rescuing the large oil painting of William Smith, founder of the College for whom the building was named, from a rear wall of the auditorium stage. In addition to the valuable painting, four mahogany chairs located on the auditorium stage and a chapel Bible were pulled from the fire.

Heavy winds from the south steered the flames in the direction of the new $50,000 gymnasium. Local firemen, sensing that Smith Hall could not be saved, turned a water hose onto the gym and, aided by the continuing snowfall, kept a second structure from catching fire.

As daybreak revealed, all that remained of William Smith Hall—only nine years old and the architectural and academic centerpiece of the campus—was a smoldering shell of brick and granite. The entire roof was missing. Spectators could stand at the rear of the structure and see clear to the other side through frameless windows.

To a writer for *The Enterprise*, a county newspaper, Smith Hall resembled "one of the ruined piles of French and Belgian masonry that stand in the path of the German army in their march through those war-devastated countries."

The financial loss of William Smith Hall was put at $71,000 ($53,000 would be recovered by insurance). Except for the few items saved, everything else inside was destroyed. Classroom desks and chairs, dozens of settees, shelves, cabinets, tables, roll-top desks and reading tables—most of them oak or maple—were reduced to ashes.

The blaze was so intense that eight class shields—metal plaques listing the names of past graduating class members—had been twisted into almost unrecognizable lumps. (Within days after the fire, Cain, with all the other demands now upon him, sent personal notes to alumni asking if they would pay to replace the shields.)

Because Smith Hall was the heart and brains of the campus, it housed under one roof all the accoutrements that make a college. And all were lost: a dozen microscopes and other apparatus essential to biological and chemical inquiry in the laboratories; display cabinets and 500 books in the bookstore; 125 hymnals and an upright piano in the auditorium; a mineral display case and a bust of George Washington in the corridor; 100 tons of coal and a heating pump in the basement; school stationary, filing cabinets, clocks, rugs and a dozen framed pictures in the administrative offices; volumes of books worth $3,500 in the library.

Those items could be replaced. What could not were records and artifacts unique to Washington College. Despite the burning of the original College building and all its contents in 1827, school officials and friends had managed to accumulate some important documents pertaining to the institution's founding. An old ledger, discovered in a waterfront warehouse in town and presented to the College, contained a list of the original subscribers and the amount they pledged to establishing the school. Cain himself had original issues of the 1789 *Philadelphia Gazette* and *Saturday Evening Post* that contained accounts of the presentation by the school of an honorary degree to George Washington. Since 1889, the school had maintained records of students and alumni. All went up in flames.

There were personal losses, too. For the past twenty-five years, Cain had been collecting notes for a financial history of the United Sates he intended to write. His labors went up in smoke.

Before the ashes of Smith Hall cooled, Cain and the trustees, who had discussed routine College business in Cain's office until ten o'clock the night of the fire, held an emergency meeting in the gymnasium. The group quickly agreed to rebuild Smith Hall as soon as possible. In the meantime, the gym would be outfitted as temporary administration headquarters, and classes would be held, if necessary, in the old wooden gym. The board also agreed to suspend classes and send students home. The fire destroyed the heating plant, and the Hill dorms were too cold for comfort. Students were to return in two weeks when a new system was expected to be in operation. Looking ahead to June, Cain concluded that commencement would have to be held in the gym.

(By the time the students returned to campus, the new gym housed an office and three recitation rooms. The old gym was refitted for two more recitation rooms, a laboratory was set up in the basement of East Hall and a reading room was prepared in Normal Hall.)

Desiring the advice and help of the College community at large, the College sent notices to alumni over the signature of James A. Pierce, the Board chairman, asking them to attend an emergency meeting in Baltimore's Rennert Hotel on January 28. "This is the greatest crisis in the affairs of the college during the memory of any man now living," the elderly Pearce wrote.

Even before the fire, Pearce, son of the late Senator Pearce and a student of the College preparatory department in 1853, had spoken of resigning from the Board. He had been appointed to the vacancy created by his father's death in 1863 and had been active in College matters ever since. He agreed to stay on during the rebuilding period, but on occasion the stress of not knowing if the Maryland legislature would continue to aid the College wore down his stamina. "We must recognize and the State must recognize that we are essentially a State College—dependent on the State for actual existence," Pearce wrote in July to fellow trustee Harry J. Hopkins of Annapolis. "Personally, at my age, I cannot continue to bear the strain and responsibility of constant harassing debt," he added.

Hopkins, who was president of the Farmers National Bank, tried to reassure Pearce. He wrote: "I realize that our College is in a very crucial period of existence. We have had many set-backs, but when you stop and consider for a moment the Institution it is today, and what it was a few years ago, there is awakened in my heart and mind the utmost gratitude and delight at the progress that has been made."

College officials, no doubt, at first were reminded of the winter fire ninety years earlier that destroyed the first school building. Raising funds for a new structure proved to be so difficult a task that the College was without a permanent home for seventeen years.

Pearce's worries about college finances were not entirely groundless. Newspaper articles in *The* (Baltimore) *Sun* in early 1916 questioned the wisdom of the legislature giving money to Washington College, St. Johns College and other private schools around the state. The paper noted that of the 126 students enrolled in Washington College, fifty-one were residents of Kent County with many others from nearby Eastern Shore counties. "It is reasonable to ask whether it is sound public policy for a large sum of the money of the whole people be devoted to the maintenance of a college which serves principally the people of one small county and its immediate environs," wrote *The Sun*.

Variations of that argument and its periodic success at swaying legislative appropriations had plagued Washington College for more that a century. But in 1916 state lawmakers approved expenditures to the College totaling $28,275 for maintenance and $10,000 for helping rebuild Smith Hall for each of the next two years.

Cain was so busy dealing with contractors, insurance agents and salvage collectors and preparing for commencement that he arranged to have a substitute take over his teaching responsibilities. If keeping the school running under those conditions was not burden enough, Cain was faced with another fire of sorts—criticism by some students of how the Chestertown volunteer firemen handled the January 16 blaze was threatening town-gown relations.

In an account of the burning of Smith Hall carried in the February issue of the student publication *The Collegian*, firefighters were blamed in part for not getting the situation under control.

"About an hour after the alarm had been given, some firemen arrived pulling a hose truck," the article reported. "One truck had apparently been left at the lower end of the campus by some who were apparently more anxious to witness the glorious sight than to aid in extinguishing the fire. There was absolutely no system in the work of the volunteer firemen of Chestertown; every one was a boss, some did not know what to do themselves, and were nervously suggesting what should be done by others. Some of the students got the hose truck which had been left by some over-enthusiast at the foot of campus, and brought it where it could be of some use."

The article continued: "To cap the climax of this regrettable inefficiency on the part of the Chestertown firemen, after the hose had been adjusted to the water plug, it was discovered that the plug wrench had been mislaid. Finally, after a series of circular movements, a wrench was supplied from an automobile, which was standing nearby."

Determined not to infringe upon *The Collegian's* editorial prerogatives, Cain wrote the publication a letter designed to soothe both sides. "If the town apparatus seemed slow in arriving, it should be borne in mind that the hour was most unfavorable for the quick assembling of men, and that perhaps our anxiety made the time seem longer that it actually was," he wrote. "If there appeared to be a lack of a directive hand may this not have been due to the belief that, the College being a community in itself, some one in authority in the College, myself perhaps, should direct the work."

The next issue of *The Collegian* carried an editorial note commending the fire department.

Bad luck seemed to follow Dr. Cain that year, even when he traveled in October to Baltimore to attend the Washington-Gallaudet football game, which Washington lost. Cain was struck by a car owned by the Monumental Brewing Company. Slightly shaken and bruised, he was helped across the street to the Rennert Hotel where he dusted himself off.

By December construction of the new William Smith Hall had reached the first floor and Cain, anxious that work was not moving as quickly as he had hoped, urged the contractor to employ more men.

The rebuilding of a nearly identical Smith Hall included two features not in the original structure. One walk-in safe was installed on the first floor and another in the basement. And on the roof a cupola was built. While the work progressed on Smith Hall under a contract with Henry S. Ripple, a new heating plant was erected and outfitted on a new and separate building by contractor Clarence E. Stubbs. The final cost of the entire project, including a $3,500 hot water system for the gym and the dormitories, was $76,000.

In early February 1918, students and the administration moved into the new William Smith Hall. On the morning of June 19, the College witnessed its first commencement in the new structure.

WHAT CAUSED THE FIRE that destroyed William Smith Hall and nearly its entire contents in 1916?

Initial appraisals suggested spontaneous combustion in a pile of coal stored near the basement furnace. A small fire had been discovered and extinguished earlier in the same area. But subsequent events on campus and around town that year turned toward pyromania.

After nightfall on March 21, fire was discovered in the new gymnasium basement. The Chestertown Fire Company arrived and extinguished the blaze, which had begun in a closet. The basement was heavily damaged.

Ten days later, a third fire raised smoke alarms on campus. Two students in Middle Hall smelled smoke and discovered a small blaze in a pile of blankets that had been placed upon a mattress in a storeroom. The fire was put out and College officials immediately hired a night watchman at $1.50 a day.

In his April 6 report to the Board of Visitors and Governors, President Cain wrote: "Evidence was found in connection with the fire in Middle Hall that shows beyond a doubt that it was the work of an incendiary. I am now convinced that the fire in the Gymnasium originated in the same manner, and probably the fire in William Smith Hall also."

Local authorities arrested a man who was suspected of setting fires at seven locations about the county. Although he was found guilty of arson and sent to jail, none of the convictions was related to the mysterious College fires.

The Water Tower Comes Down

MARSHALL WILLIAMS

CHESTERTOWN'S OLD WATER TOWER, now dismantled, was more closely associated with Washington College than with the town. Built in 1915, the handsome eighty-foot-tall tower was erected on College Hill to take advantage of its situation as the highest point in town. In 1915 the tower was a lonely structure hovering over farmhouses and cornfields. In later years it was crowded by an expanding campus. Finally, with the removal of Gibson Avenue and construction of the new Eugene B. Casey Academic Center, the water tower was squeezed out of existence.

In its seventy-five years the water tower was a friendly and helpful neighbor for townspeople and college students alike. For local citizens returning from a trip, the water tower was the first sign that Chestertown was near, and many families would make a game of who would be the first to see the tower.

For college students, the tower served as a billboard to advertise athletic scores, fraternity symbols and all manner of friendly and not-so-friendly messages. An important rite of passage for many students was to climb the tower's ladder to the platform encircling the tank.

The reward was an unparalleled view of the college, the town and the Chester's sweep from Henderson's Wharf to Devil's Reach.

The very brave student would climb two additional ladders straddling the tank to reach the tower's highest point. Few if any would stand on the silver ball at the very top, but sitting was not impossible. Silk parachutes, water bombs, hats and chickens are just some of the things that were launched from the tower. Banners were draped from the top, and deer carcasses were hung from its lower girders by student hunters.

In the 1930s, '40s and '50s, football and baseball scores dominated the water tower, and everyone knew they could get the latest news of WC's exploits on the field—both home and away—by checking the tower. During World War II the prevailing message was, "Kilroy Was Here." Later, tower decorations ran to fraternity advertisements, and the Sigs most adventurously made a habit of climbing to the very top of the tower and painting a message that could be seen only by airplane.

The water tower held 120,000 gallons, or nearly 500 tons of water. It was a necessary part of the town's water system, maintaining adequate pressure as well as enough water to fight fires and provide for other emergencies. According to Medford Capel, superintendent of the town's water system, when the steam-operated canneries were active, they depended on the tower's capacity to produce the canned fruits and vegetables for which the region was famous. The town had the tower painted by hand every ten years or so. The tower's replacement is a million-gallon holding tank near the Upper Shore Community Health Center off Scheeler Lane, north of Chestertown.

Asked if the water tower was ever blocked or unable to supply water, Capel laughed and said, "The water supply's never been interrupted, but there was a baseball game interrupted once because of the water tower. A man named Bob Penn—a 'local yokel,' he had a hell of a lot of nerve and was ornery as hell, he went up the tower during a ball game, climbed right to he top—there was a large ball on top of the tower at that time—and he stood on his head right on top of the ball on the tower. Stopped the baseball game. That was sixty years ago."

Bob Penn's stunt wasn't matched in sixty years, but others pulled clever pranks. One WC student in the 1950s taped a walkie-talkie at the top of the tower and frightened passersby with threats of "I'm going to jump, I'm going to jump." The police and fire department arrived and eventually discovered the hoax; the prankster was never caught.

Perhaps the most provocative writing on the tower was in the turbulent years of desegregation in the early 1960s. Volunteer Freedom Riders, college students canvassing Southern towns promoting desegregation, found some sympathizers at the college when they arrived on the Eastern Shore. Disgruntled segregationists climbed the tower with additional ladders and diligently printed "Booker T. Washington College" in perfect lettering over one side of the tower.

Retired buildings and grounds supervisor Bill Coleman grew up in the shadow of the water tower. "They'd pump up the tower from the pump down on Kent Street," Coleman remembers, "and the tower had an overflow pipe. When it was full, the water would start running over, and we'd have to call up the town and say 'the water tower's running over.' Every Christmas, they'd send us a box of candy for calling to say the water tower was running over."

How vital was the water tower to the academic life of Washington College? Former Alumni Director Pat Trams '75 remembers a science professor asking students to determine the circumference of the water tower as a physics problem. After puzzling over the seemingly impossible task, Trams came up with what she thought was a perfect solution—she climbed the tower and measured the tank with a tape.

The water tower inspired budding writers as well. Nicholas Nappo '81 recently wrote to the *Washington College Magazine* describing a poem he wrote as a freshman: "To a star-struck freshman like myself … the already imposing water tower took on mythic proportions. On the flat campus it caught first sun and last light; like a great Oscar it seemed to symbolize all that my friends and I hoped for in the way of literary excellence; its sky-scraping graffiti spoke of daring feats achieved long before I had put sharpened pencil to S.A.T."

Nappo's poem, a parody of James Dickey's poem "The Man-Child," includes the fantasy of the writer falling from the tower's height:

I who fell swiftly
From the silver structure in Kent House Yard
Where it stood mute in the pale moonlight
Waiting for dumb jokers like myself
Who, in a moment of macho
Madness seized the ladder cold
In both hands and pulled
Myself up the iron spire. Craning

Down, where the far jewels hung
Below and meshed with boxes
Of light, I saw her
Crossing the square. Leaning
My hat my gloves then too late,
Looking back up
Through the steam of my last
Breath, I saw the tower stretching
Higher and swiftly higher.

The water tower played an active role in the romantic life of WC students as well. Mike Travieso '66 described a scene with his girlfriend, classmate Bonnie Abrams, following a college dance. "We had a fight," Mike recalled, "and Bonnie and I were real mad with each other. So to protest, I climbed up the tower—I'd never climbed it before. I went all the way up, to the ball on top, and started yelling Bonnie's name over the campus. I guess her friends went to get her, and she came out and got me to come down, and we made up."

Chas Foster '89 climbed the water tower many times, experimenting with graffiti, posters and banners hung from the side. He would gallantly offer to paint women's names up on the tower, and after seeing the movie *Ferris Bueller's Day Off*, which featured the line "Ferris Bueller is a Righteous Dude," Chas fashioned a spray-paint holder out of a broom handle with lengths of string carefully attached to activate the paint can. He made it as far as "Cathy Jewell is a Righteous B…" when the string broke. Rather than embarrass or anger his girlfriend with this questionable, unfinished statement, Chas climbed up and stood on the top of the railing that encircled the tower to complete his message. "I guess that was pretty stupid," he says looking back on this foolish bravery. "And anyway, Cathy said the whole thing was pretty stupid. She would deny that it was about her. She'd tell people, 'that's not me; that's another Cathy Jewell that's written up there.'"

Three students claimed to be the last to climb the water tower. On Wednesday night, April 11, 1990, Don Steele, Jeff Huebeck and Mike Gauchet climbed the tower ladder up to the tank, which had already lost its roof. They fondly touched the belly of the tank and climbed back down. "It was one of the best," says Don Steele. "When we got down we saw a window open in the new Academic Center. We went inside and climbed up to the cupola, where the view is almost as good as from the tower. We thought maybe we'd started a new tradition." By the end of the next day the water tower had been dismantled.

The Chestertown water tower is remembered with fondness by many. The organizing committee for the seventieth reunion of Chestertown High School's Class of 1920 asked the *Kent County News* to provide some photographs of the water tower to display during reunion. "They simply wanted the photos as remembrances of an old friend," said former *News* editor H. Hurtt Deringer '59, who climbed the water tower many times and often used it in college sports photographs to frame lacrosse and soccer action.

Somehow, no one was ever hurt climbing the water tower. Perhaps one reason its dismantling caused the outcry it did among students, alumni and neighbors was that the tower was always a friendly accomplice to the exploits and shenanigans of the tower climbers and self-described artists. For many, the tower was a lucky charm watching benignly and knowingly over the college campus and Chestertown for more than seventy-five years.

The Chestertown Blast

NICOLE VATTIMO

THE MORNING WAS sunny and still, and the temperature had climbed into the eighties long before the sun could make it to the top of the sky. Children played in yards and rode their bikes on nearly empty streets. There was little traffic at this time, which was common in those days in a country town where adults were already at work. Then, as clocks ticked 10:25, a mighty boom shook Chestertown.

As a dark mushroom of smoke formed over the northeast corner of town, there came another boom. Minutes later, again, boom. And again, boom, four explosions separated only by minutes—shattering windows along High Street from Radcliffe Mill all the way to the waterfront. Sirens began to wail. Some people ran from their homes and businesses, scrambling into their cars to get out of town. Others rushed toward the tower of smoke to look for loved ones. They found there a horror never imagined. The northeast section of Chestertown was destroyed. Kent Manufacturing Company—one of the town's largest employers—was gone. Where it stood was now flame and smoke and rubble.

As the day of July 16, 1954, came to a close, the death toll was reported at eleven. Those quickly identified were Nelson Lord, Mary

Fallowfield, Nellie Starr, Tina Mae Taylor, Magdaline Seiler and Eva Fisher. Days passed before sad and anxious families could be sure of the identities of the other five bodies: Ida Mench, Marguerite Batchelor, Betty Marie Wheedleton, Mary Covington and Barbara Rockermann. The hospital overflowed while the staff struggled to treat another fifty people injured during the day. Patients suffering burns, cuts, broken bones and shock lay on blankets on sidewalks around the hospital.

The explosions went on from 10:25 to 10:40 that morning. Fearing more blasts, authorities advised people in the vicinity of the plant to evacuate their homes. Traffic backed up over the Chester River Bridge and rescue squads had to force their way through lines of cars to reach the scene and treat those injured.

Kent Manufacturing Company—one of the first large businesses to open in Chestertown after nearly a century of slow economic decline—originally was devoted to making detonators for the government during World War II. It started up in 1941, hiring a workforce of 350, of which eighty percent were female. Owners were the then-mayor of Chestertown, Philip Wilmer, along with his associates: Charles Eshman, Tony Fabrizi, and Joseph H. McLain, then a professor of chemistry at Washington College. With a monthly payroll of approximately $50,000, the plant was a major asset in Chestertown's economy, and it played an important role in the lives of the women who worked there. Up to that time on the Eastern Shore, few women earned regular paychecks and, with their men at war, it was necessary for mothers, sisters and daughters to support their families.

Ann Wilmer Hoon, the mayor's daughter, recalled that on one occasion a friend of hers employed by the plant walked up and held out her palm, holding a dollar in quarters. The woman told Hoon this was the first money she had ever earned on her own. However, as the war wound down and the need for munitions diminished, people worried that the jobs would be lost. To the town's relief, the plant's doors remained open as it shifted production to the making of fireworks. The plant had minor accidents over the years, resulting in a couple of small fires, but no one supposed what was in store for the factory and its staff in July of 1954.

In a town gathering held on October 28, 2004, for those who wanted to learn more about the blasts, Maynard Porter, the plant's supervisor, explained: "Towards the end of the war, one of the owners of the plant had been in the fireworks business, so they brought the business to the plant. At the time of the explosion the plant was reworking M80s, and the first explosion occurred in my building in the tunnel [where the M80s were placed to dry]. The first explosion was small; I was away from my building at this time. After the first, I made my way back towards my building, and just as I got back the furnace room exploded. What had gone off was a pile of M80s that were being stored; how exactly these ignited was never answered."

In an interview on the day of the explosions, then-Fire Chief Alex Herzberg told reporters he believed vibrations from two jet bombers that flew over the plant a few moments before the explosions began were responsible for the tragedy. Though people did remember planes flying over at the time of the accident, this was never proved to be the cause of the explosions.

The U.S. Fireworks web page explains a little about the dangerous nature of the material the women and men of Kent Manufacturing Company were working with. The original M80 was a military simulator that was sold as a firecracker. M80s are red in color, and a little smaller than a shot glass, with a diameter of 5/8 of an inch. They also contain a green waterproof fuse, which protrudes from the side. The original M80s that Kent Manufacturing Company worked with contained two grams of flash powder and over the years were responsible for hundreds of serious injuries due to its powerful blast.

A dozen years after the Chestertown blasts, in 1966, these items were banned by the U.S. Consumer Product Safety Commission. The Federal Bureau of Alcohol, Tobacco and Firearms made them illegal in the 1970s. Today, legal M80s contain 50 milligrams of flash powder, about 1/40th of the original M80.

The explosions at the Chestertown plant made headlines all over the United States. The *Kent County News* reported that President Eisenhower ordered Katherine Howard, deputy director of the Federal Civil Defense

Administration, to fly to Chestertown. Several days later the *Washington Post* reported, "Because the plant was operating in part under defense contracts, FBI agents and Army counter intelligence corps officers were dispatched to Chestertown to check on the possibility of sabotage."

Ann Hoon recalls, "This tragedy was heard of all over. I even have newspapers from Hawaii that give detailed reports of what was going on here in our small town. It's extraordinary."

Willis Wells, who was the undertaker for four of the women killed in the blast, remembers: "I was near the site when the last explosion happened. The streets were deserted. The women running from the plant were hysterical. I remember seeing some frantically climbing the fences to get off the facility. They had no clue what was happening; I remember such a sense of panic among everyone. There were no rescue squads there at first; I took sedans and converted them into transportation for invalids. I was one of the first inside the wreckage that was left after the blasts; all I could see around me was rubble and smoke. Some people escaped, but there were bodies still left inside the remains of the burning buildings.

"One woman had run to the other side of Radcliffe Creek to try and escape, and I remember picking her up and taking her to the hospital. The hospital was packed, and it was so sad to see some of the women having to wait on blankets outside, until someone could tend to them. I made three trips to the armory that day, which was converted into a morgue during the disaster. The four I acted as undertaker for were unrecognizable, their bodies were so charred, but from jewelry we discovered who they were."

Wells said that several women, whom he did not care to name, spoke up after the event, expressing how upset they were that a plant containing dangerous material was built within such close proximity to the town.

At the October meeting in 2004, Ruth Creighton remembered with tears in her eyes what little she could: "My grandmother was one of the five unidentified. I remember my mother telling me down through the years how after the explosion they went into town searching and hoping that she had amnesia and had simply wandered off. They searched in the marsh and the woods, hoping they would find her or her remains; those are my only memories."

John Henry Myers thinks back to the day of the explosion and shakes his head, saying, "They originally converted the plant to fireworks because it was a moneymaker. The town did not know the danger of the explosives that were being stored there, even some of the people working there didn't know. The danger was not talked about a lot in those days, because they did not want people to be scared to work there, and it was one of the biggest employers of its time. After the explosion, when they found out the danger of how many explosives the plant held, they decided they didn't want it so close to the town and so never rebuilt it. There were some people who had hard feelings towards the mayor when they found out how many explosives were held there without their knowledge. I mean, had the main stash gone off it would have wiped out Chestertown."

Today one would never know what happened on the site years ago. The northeastern end of High Street contains Chestertown's bustling Industrial Park, home to a concrete plant.

Ann Hoon recalled that her father felt tremendous guilt for many years after the accident, not knowing how to deal with the fact that women—his employees and friends—had been killed at his plant. Noting that fewer people who were affected by the event are still alive today, she says, "We need this event recorded because it was an important element of Chestertown's history. It should not be forgotten just because time has passed."

Town Manager Bill Ingersoll says, "I wish I could say safety and zoning laws were instituted, but the reality is that laws regarding that sort of thing did not come into play until the early 1970s, when some of the first zoning restrictions were developed. I will say that Maryland fireworks laws got stricter in the time after the explosion."

Chestertown got a scary reminder of its past in 1979, when it began to build the Industrial Park. Ingersoll says, "As the construction crew began to dig on the site, they hit buried pyrotechnics with their machines. Even tough construction workers were not going to stick around to watch another episode like the one in 1954. Experts from

Aberdeen [Proving Ground] were called in and they removed the material, which was probably wreckage left over from Kent Manufacturing Company. But everyone was a little nervous to work around the site after that, and people certainly remembered what had happened in that spot years before."

Having Set the Clocks Forward

MARY WOOD

This is the hour I must lose:
an infant morning
screened behind budding arrowheaded leaves.

The blue and silver river
weaves towards the Chesapeake,
a net capturing the shore.

Birds wake up singing,
flinging songs from the tree tops
into the ear of dawn.

This is the hour, that
will not come again,
until November tramples the leaves.

End of the Line

JOHN A. BUETTNER

A JOGGER OR dog-walker crossing Kudner Bridge behind Washington College's athletic fields is unlikely to realize that the weed-choked ravine there conceals what was once Chestertown's route to the nation's steel thruway of commerce. For all of you stuck on today's information superhighway, that's a railroad.

Now it is as undeniable as it is unbelievable, but Chestertown was once, quite literally, the center of the United States.

According to the 1790 census, the first taken in the new nation, Chestertown and environs—literally the coordinates 39.16.30 by 76.11.12—represented the population center of the country. There is no marker, no monument, no sign*; so perhaps it was the magnetism of this mysterious spot that spawned, as John C. Hayman wrote in his book *Rails Along the Chesapeake: A History of Railroading on the Delmarva Peninsula*, the "delusions of grandeur" that brought the railroad to Kent County and ultimately to Chestertown.

*Although the exact geographic spot of the population center of the nation as determined by the 1790 census remains unmarked, Chestertown does acknowledge its unusual status with a plaque located at the Town Hall building on Cross Street.

"While most railroads had their pet plans for expansion, there was one upper Shore line which always seemed to have delusions of grandeur which were never quite fulfilled. In fact, it undertook so many different projects throughout its history that it's practically impossible to record them all. This line was originally the Kent County Railroad."

Despite these grand plans, the train arrived late. Chestertown did not see a line into the town until 1872, well after the Civil War and three years after the driving of the Golden Spike at Ogden, Utah, completed the first transcontinental railroad. In those post-Civil War years, railroad entrepreneurs were as numerous as the dot-commers of the 1990s. With maps, surveys and charters, their railroads were often little more than paper entities offering more promise than substance. This was to be the case with the Kent County Railroad's grand plans.

In the original plan of the Kent County Railroad, Chestertown was somewhat of an afterthought, a small branch on a trunk to be passed by in favor of Rock Hall and Tolchester. The lofty goal was "to form what would have been the first trans-peninsula railroad," writes Hayman—a line straddling two states, reaching bay to bay, Delaware to Chesapeake. Unlike Chestertown, the bayside towns of Rock Hall and Tolchester had deep water and easier access to larger ports and commercial centers, such as Baltimore.

"Chestertown was, of course, also a port of some importance, but its location far up the Chester River made for a long steamer trip to Baltimore and the desire for a bay terminal," Hayman adds. Frequent financial problems and the neglect of absentee railroad tycoons thwarted these plans. Luckily, the bypass never happened—Chestertown became the end of line.

By the time the railroad came to Chestertown, the town was no longer the center of the country nor of any particular importance in the nation's transportation infrastructure. It was, as the late railroad historian Frank Donovan, wrote in 1947, "The Land of the Branch Line Local."

In 1900, the giant Pennsylvania Railroad acquired what was then called the Baltimore and Delaware Bay Railroad (the former Kent County Railroad), firmly entrenching the little line in the Pennsy's vast

24 | **CLAYTON TO OXFORD—SOUTHWARD**

STATIONS	↑481 DAILY EX. SUN.	483 SUNDAY ONLY	↑485 SAT. ONLY	↑479 DAILY EX. SAT. AND SUN.
Leave	A.M.	A.M.	P.M.	P.M.
CLAYTON	S 8.50	S 8.25	S 1.47	S 5.06
KENTON	S 8.59	S 8.34		
HARTLY	S 9.07	F 8.41	F 2.01	F 5.19
HART	9.08	8.42	2.02	5.20
MARYDEL	S 9.16	F 8.50	F 2.09	F 5.26
HENDERSON	S 9.21	F 8.57	F 2.14	F 5.31
GOLDSBORO	S 9.28	F 9.03	F 2.19	S 5.36
GREENSBORO	F 9.38	F 9.12	F 2.25	F 5.41
PET	9.39	9.13	2.26	5.42
RIDGELY	S 9.48	S 9.22	S 2.33	S 5.49
QUEEN ANNE	S 9.57	S 9.30	F 2.40	F 5.55
ANNE	9.58	9.31	2.41	5.56
CORDOVA	S 10.08	F 9.38	F 2.48	S 6.02
EASTON	S 10.39	S 10.01	S 2.56	S 6.15
EASTON JCT	10.40	10.02		
CROSS	10.41	10.03		
LLANDAFF	F 10.47	F 10.06		
TRAPPE	F 10.52	F 10.14	Will Not Run May 31, 1947	
OXFORD	S 10.59	S 10.20	Will Not Run July 6, 1947	
Arrive	A.M.	A.M.	P.M.	P.M.
	↑481	483	↑485	↑479

OXFORD TO CLAYTON—NORTHWARD

STATIONS	↑478	↑480	482
Arrive	A.M.	P.M.	P.M.
CLAYTON	S 7.45	S 5.04	S 7.43
KENTON		S 4.55	
HARTLY	F 7.32	S 4.45	F 7.29
HART	7.29	4.43	7.28
MARYDEL	F 7.23	S 4.36	F 7.21
HENDERSON	F 7.18	4.29	
GOLDSBORO	F 7.13	F 4.21	F 7.18
GREENSBORO	F 7.06	S 4.12	F 7.05
PET	7.04	4.04	7.04
RIDGELY	S 6.59	S 3.58	S 6.57
QUEEN ANNE	F 6.52	S 3.48	6.49
ANNE	6.51	3.48	6.47
CORDOVA	F 6.46	S 3.37	F 6.42
EASTON	S 6.34	S 3.28	6.30
EASTON JCT		3.11	6.24
CROSS		3.10	6.23
LLANDAFF	Will Not Run May 31, 1947	S 3.06	6.19
TRAPPE	July 5 1947	S 3.02	6.13
OXFORD		S 2.55	6.05
			Will Run Sept. 1, 1947 Will Not Run Aug. 31, 1947
Leave	A.M.	P.M.	P.M.
	DAILY EX. SUN.	DAILY EX. SUN.	SUNDAY ONLY
	↑478	↑480	482

Train No. 481 is superior by direction to Train No. 480.
Train No. 483 is superior by direction to Train No. 482.
Train No. 485 is superior by direction to Train No. 480.
Train No. 479 is superior by direction to Trains No. 480 and No. 482.

Del. Divn. G. O. 705—2.01 A.M.—6-22-47.

TOWNSEND TO CHESTERTOWN—SOUTHWARD | **25**

STATIONS	*471 DAILY EX. SUN.	↑473 SUNDAY ONLY
Leave	A.M.	A.M.
TOWNSEND	S 8.25	S 8.15
VANDYKE	F 8.31	S 8.21
GOLT	F 8.37	S 8.27
MASS	8.44	S 8.32
MASSEY	S 9.19	S 8.34
LAMBSON	F 9.26	S 8.41
BLACK	F 9.32	S 8.47
KENNEDYVILLE	S 9.39	S 8.54
KEN	9.40	8.58
STILL POND	F 9.44	F 8.59
LYNCH	F 9.48	F 9.03
WORTON	F 9.53	F 9.08
CHESTERTOWN	S 10.35	S 9.19
Arrive	A.M.	A.M.
	*471	↑473

CHESTERTOWN TO TOWNSEND—NORTHWARD

STATIONS	*470	↑472
Arrive	P.M.	P.M.
TOWNSEND	S 5.35	S 6.50
VANDYKE	F 5.17	F 6.44
GOLT	F 5.15	F 6.39
MASS	5.06	6.33
MASSEY	S 5.08	S 6.32
LAMBSON	F 4.55	F 6.24
BLACK	F 4.45	F 6.20
KENNEDYVILLE	S 4.36	S 6.13
KEN	4.32	6.12
STILL POND	F 4.25	F 6.08
LYNCH	F 4.22	F 6.04
WORTON	F 4.16	F 6.00
CHESTERTOWN	S 4.00	S 5.45
Leave	P.M.	P.M.
	DAILY EX. SUN.	SUNDAY ONLY
	*470	↑472

Train No. 471 is superior by direction to Train No. 470.

In the late 1940s, passenger traffic on the Pennsylvania Railroad's Chestertown Branch was rapidly disappearing, down to just two trains per day—one inbound, one outbound—with most of the line's stations designated as flagstops.

rail transportation network from New York to Chicago. Old Southern sympathies aside, Chestertown now looked northward, tied into the ebb and flow of railroad traffic controlled from the Pennsy's Philadelphia headquarters. But its branch line character was left fully intact.

Chestertown's railroad architecture was the simple design of the typical multitasking branch line: a terminal passenger station, sidings for freight, a small freight station and a wye—a track configuration of three turnouts (switches, to lay people) that allows a locomotive (or an entire train) to reverse itself without the need for a turntable by performing a three-point turn. Chestertown's wye occupied what is now the Industrial Park on upper High Street.

Living in "The Land of the Branch Line Local" is slow and easy. And so are the trains. Chestertown's schedules were light on the eyes, just four passenger trains per day—two in and two out. If you wanted to get somewhere, you didn't expect to get there quickly. As Donovan wrote of traveling to Chestertown by rail in *Trains* magazine (February 1947):

> One of the peculiarities of branch line travel is that you commit yourself entirely to the hands of the railroad. It may be decreed by the timecard that you lay over a half hour or half a day at a lonely junction or obscure terminus. If you take it philosophically and in good spirit you'll get all the enjoyment Walt Whitman did out of his unplotted meanderings. At any rate, Chestertown is an attractive community beautifully situated on the bank of the river from which it takes its name. The green, well-kept campus of Washington College, the many old southern mansions, and the graceful weeping willows along the waterfront beckon the visitor.

A typical passenger and mail run on the 29-mile line to Chestertown, from the Townsend, Delaware, junction with the Pennsylvania Railroad's Delmarva Secondary mainline, was about two hours and ten minutes. Weekdays, that is. The locals affectionately—and sarcastically—called the train "The Bullet."

"People knew about irony in those days," says Ralph Thornton, a 1940 graduate of Washington College. After college and military service during World War II, he worked for *The News Journal* in Wilmington and often used "The Bullet" to visit his parents in Chestertown. In those waning days of passenger service on the Pennsylvania's Delmarva Division, that was a three-hour trip by rail with the long layovers that typified branch line travel. The railroad gave you plenty of downtime to think, to contemplate the virtue of patience or invent a new pastime.

"We would sit and wait, and wait, until the schedule said it was time to leave," he remembers. "So while we were waiting, the crew would get off the train and pitch horse shoes alongside the track."

A typical train during a weekday run was a "mixed train," a usual sight on rural branch lines: a passenger car, a combo car carrying baggage, mail and passengers, and a few freight cars destined for delivery to businesses along the line or to be returned to the junction.

Sundays were faster—passenger service only—about an hour and five minutes from Chestertown to Townsend. But the Pennsylvania's Sunday runs ran afoul of some of the town's fathers. These faster trains were well patronized by the locals, to the consternation of some of Chestertown's clergy, who thought the railroad's Sunday service reduced attendance at the Lord's Sunday service.

In 1906, when the Pennsylvania inaugurated the Sunday runs, many of Chestertown's moral leaders petitioned the mighty Pennsy to put an end to it. On May 12, 1906, the editor of the *Kent County News* opined: "The inauguration of the Sunday trains to Chestertown will not in any way help the moral tone of our community." Nevertheless, the Standard Railroad of the World had its way.

Strangely enough, by 1937, the Pennsylvania Railroad was filing its own petition, too, but this one was to the federal government to eliminate passenger and mail service to Chestertown and all intermediate stations along the line. Branch lines rarely supported a density of traffic to make them profitable operations, and the railroad had being seeing red far too long on the Chestertown Branch. Protests and appeals to the state and federal government from local businesses put a halt to the abandonment, and the weekday passenger and mail service limped along for another twelve years.

AT THE END of the Chestertown branch of the Pennsylvania, the railroad was a routine life—and a circus parade of curiosities. It mostly depended upon your age at the time.

In its heyday during the early 20th century, the railroad served a small but bustling center of commerce and industry in Chestertown.

Arthur Culver served as Chestertown's railroad stationmaster from 1918 until 1961.

At the very end of the line on the riverfront were Hubbard's fertilizer plant and the Marvel Packing Co., a basket factory nicknamed "the Academy" because so many Washington College students worked there to supplement their incomes. Uptown, off a short branch, the American Strawboard factory manufactured special paper patterns for shipbuilding.

From Chestertown the Pennsy hauled millions of baby chicks and oysters packed in ice; tens of thousands of sheep, cows and hogs; and hundreds of Washington College students returning to college or leaving for the summer. It brought fire equipment and firefighters from Wilmington to help contain the great Chestertown Fire of 1910. Even the Frank Robinson Circus arrived by train and hauled its carnival wagons by elephants from the station to the fairgrounds on Quaker Neck Road.

"When I was a boy, we used to play down by the station and the fertilizer plant, where the tracks ended in town," recalled Thomas Davis. "There was a car dealership down there, right where Wilmer Park is now, and we saw the damnedest thing—a boxcar stacked with brand new cars in racks. Hell if I know how they got 'em in and out them boxcars!"

A milk station occupied the site where Newt's Hillside Bar now stands so Kent County dairy farmers could ship milk and cream in refrigerated cars to pasteurization plants in Philadelphia. Tomatoes were shipped by rail, bound for Northeastern markets. Day laborers earned one cent for every basket loaded.

The station was more than a place to catch a train or some gossip, it was Chestertown's connection to the world. From the station, Washington College football scores were teletyped to the Baltimore papers, Western Union telegrams were sent and received, and many Washington College coeds' long-distance romances were maintained by the stationmaster's telegraph.

Of course, the railroad brought the sundry items of mail and eagerly awaited express packages to the merchants and citizens of the town.

"The contact that you had with people, well you knew everybody and everybody knew you," remembered the late Arthur Culver, Chestertown's stationmaster from 1918 to 1961, in a 1983 interview. Even some of the day laborers who delivered packages that arrived at the station "couldn't read a word but never made a mistake," recounted Culver.

"When I started working for Fox's variety store on High Street, we used to get a lot of shoes and things from Baltimore and they'd come by train," says Anna E. Cole, a businesswoman in Chestertown for more than thirty years. "We'd come down to the depot to pick them up from Mr. Culver. I still remember him with all his slips and baggage."

Chestertown's station also mirrored the social inequities of the time. The northside of the station was the ladies' waiting room, in the middle the agent's offices, and on the southside the men's. Only the men's side had a restroom.

On July 4, 1949, the last mixed train left Chestertown. Over the next decade, Culver, who originally managed a staff of five, would become a staff of one. Passenger and mail service ended and, while freight service would continue until 1996, the salad days of the American railroad— and its neglected children, the branch lines—were long gone.

Branch lines like Chestertown's were demolished by neglect through the hamstrung finances of the major Class 1 lines such as the Pennsylvania. "The roadbed had gotten so bad by the 1970s," it was reported, "that trains were restricted to a speed of eight miles per hour" on the Chestertown line. While the outline of the branch line survived the merger of the Pennsylvania Railroad into the PennCentral Railroad, the bankruptcy of the PennCentral and a federal bailout through Conrail of the financially exhausted eastern railroads, Chestertown's railroad heydays had effectively reached the end of the line.

The departure of the last mixed train also left mixed feelings about the future of Chestertown and the world for a man like Culver, for whom "next to his wife and children, his work for the railroad was the most important thing in his life." Not just a connection to the nation's railroad infrastructure was lost. So was a way of life.

Rebirth

PAT HEROLD NIELSEN

In February, when fields are as worn as a poor monk's robe,
I search the garden for green,
And dream of daffodil, tulip, peony and rose.

Craving spring, craving the abundance of spring,
I lift mats of dead leaves, snap sticks to the ground,
And listen for birds singing a thousand miles away.

In the distance, the river is a cool blue eye—clear and insistent.
What of my spring?
What of eel and turtle, herring and shad?

What of horseshoe crab and yellow perch, or clam as round as a tear?
When you wait for spring, the river says, wait with me—
Wait with the heron's sharp gaze into drifting grass.

The Buzz on Chestertown

JOHN LANG

THE SWALLOWS THAT come back to San Juan Capistrano are famous, and it's not fair. What about a very different winged wonder of another charmed place just as rich in history and architecture and seasonal delights? Honor is overdue to the birds that gather at a crossroads there as darkness closes, like guardians of the night—such comforts to the people in their homes.

The buzzards of Chestertown. Why nobody celebrates them, I don't know.

Swallows return to Capistrano annually, which means they've got to take flight from there every year, too, and presumably go as far as they can flap, and stay away for months, or else there wouldn't be such a big deal about their returning, but you never hear any Capistranians mentioning this significant fact.

Our dedicated buzzards soar around every part of Maryland's Eastern Shore all year long but congregate by the hundreds in Chestertown in the autumn—so contented they remain throughout the worst of winters and don't abandon their eye-catching aerie until dense growth of leaves in the spring makes it impossible for them to alight. They're not squeezed in some old belfry made of cheap adobe in a faraway

California churchyard, like the swallows, either. Our discerning birds swoop down on the center of town, perching in a sort of spooky, to be perfectly honest, thicket of old-growth trees and vines sprouting from a ravine alongside the intersection of Spring and Route 213—where there's a convenient stoplight so passersby can pause and marvel.

Is that a gift of nature, or what?

There are two service stations at that intersection and a coffee shop close by serving heavy breakfasts the whole day, plus a four-chair barber shop and one of the finest Dollar General stores anywhere. So visitors could eat and get gas, shop for placemats, get a Kent County buzz cut, then take their ease strolling below hundreds of fantastically indigested—not to mention federally protected, so obviously more important than flighty swallows—buzzards.

But are town fathers and mothers taking advantage of this opportunity? Not quite yet. There's a new million-dollar tourist center only a block away with maybe a hundred brochures directing tourists to local entertainments, from the game farm where you can shoot four pheasants for $95, to the Mason Family Corn Maze (bring a flashlight after dark). Nothing points strangers to what they'd most want to inspect, probably, if only they knew it as an official tourist site: The Buzzard Roost of Chestertown.

Anybody has to admit, that's got a ring to it. There ought to be a movie and a song. And a festival in winter when the leaves are fallen and the buzzards are settled on the bare, laced limbs, their still black figures as somber as a synod of bishops. All it would take to get these projects going is a little more community spirit.

Of course our leaders are terribly busy overseeing a town of some 1200 homes with For Sale signs in front of about every tenth house. This is not because of a sad local depression, far from it. It's a realty unreality. What's happening is that Chestertown is being discovered (again), and sorry structures anyone could have had a few years ago for practically nothing are going today for multiples of five to ten. A contractor I sometimes see enjoying his good fortune at Andy's—where, yes, everybody knows your name, plus who you're kin to and approximately how much you make—bought one old wreck on High Street this year for something like $120,000, put another hundred thousand into fix-up, and flipped it a few months later for $800,000. This didn't make him a complete local hero though, because folks know: if he hadn't driven up property values by renovating half a dozen other nearby houses, he might have had that shell in the first place for $50,000.

Chestertown sure ain't what it was. Popsicle Johnson's Junkyard is a memory, and no one's seen old Carroll Gibbs, who used to walk around town with a broom, sweeping the sidewalks, for a long time. There's still that side-street trailer court, but it's not called one anymore; recently a handsome sign went up in front announcing it is AMBERLY—A Private Community [No Trespassing]. On weekends there seem to be almost as many Lexuses as pickup trucks, and more designer dogs than fat black Labs, and the one thing everybody still here by Monday is most likely to bring up is how much they might get for their house now, if only they knew of someplace else they'd rather be.

So, the day I headed to Town Hall to check on how they were coming along with their buzzard endeavors, officials had other matters on their minds, understandably, at first. Town Manager Bill Ingersoll had let himself be distracted by such things as a proposal to hugely expand the historic district and also, too, with Chestertown's 300th birthday in 2006. He seemed to me unready for the more urgent project.

"The buzzards? They're back?" He added, quickly, "They're migratory, you know."

Then he set me straight, "They are not really buzzards. They are turkey vultures. You are not supposed to call them buzzards."

Okay Bill, but anyway, how about considering Chestertown's metaphorical potentials? Who is it buying up the houses here for unbelievable prices? Rich people. And who's managed to get that rich? Old people. And why is it you see the same fixed-up houses back on the market soon enough? Dead people. Sure, the same thing is happening down in St. Michaels and Oxford, too, where retirees come in and retirees pass on, but we've got the imagery they can't touch in those burgs. We got the knock-knock, portents that are showing us the way, and the makings of an unforgettable civic campaign to let our newcomers know they've really arrived (and will soon enough depart). We got the buzzards! That is, vultures.

Ingersoll's eyes went here, went there. His smile was gone. "I'm not going to have anything at all to say about your metaphors."

Then this public official confessed to something only rumored on the far side of the Chester River in the unincorporated settlement where I live and where, a few times, the vultures have congregated, pecking on our roofs and pooping on our boats, which eats holes in our bimini tops. On several occasions, Ingersoll admitted, efforts have been made in Chestertown to shoo its indigenous symbols of vainglory out of the town where they rightly belong.

"Then they fly across the river and settle on the houses there, and they eat the little rocks off the roofing materials. Need 'em for their craws," he added, and his smile was definitely back.

Not, Ingersoll was quick to say, that town officials officially do anything to drive away their buzzards. No, but one time the residents around Eliason Hollow, the gloomy grove where the birds customarily roost, were surveyed to see if they thought the flock unsightly and wanted it gone. To the town manager's surprise, seventy-five percent of the folks didn't mind. It was just a few individuals who got noisemakers and ruffled the stinking feathers.

As Ingersoll explained it, you can get a permit for this after proving the birds a nuisance, and then after firing off noisemakers for a month you're allowed to shoot one. You're supposed to hang the carcass where the other buzzards can see it for another full month, except if they eat it, and after that you can shoot one more.

People who live the closest to Eliason Hollow, however, didn't admit doing any such thing. John Parker, who manages the fine Parker House B&B on the west side of the woods, does acknowledge banging metal poles together sometimes. "They'd fly away, and they'd fly right back," he says. The buzzards don't settle on his property, and they're really no bother to his B&B, says Parker. Still, he can get aggravated. "Everybody in town, everywhere I go, it's what they always say to me, 'Hi, John, how are the buzzards doing?'" Parker has counted as many as 150 vultures at a time in those trees next door, and he's made one ecological discovery: "They sure [relieve themselves] a lot. They go feed during the day on dead fish along the river and by three or four o'clock they're back in those trees. That's all they do, they sit up there and [relieve themselves]. You might want to clean this up," he suggested.

Outside the north border of the grove is the beautifully restored Victorian-style Stam House (formerly Hills Inn), which, before Michael and Marta Girone bought it five years ago, was locally known as The Addams Family Mansion because of sagging porches, dangling shutters, collapsed ceilings and a big dead tree filled with buzzards.

"They're gone from the place now, but before we moved in they were all over," Marta says. "When we were working on the tower, putting in a skylight, once I heard a plop sound and looked up. It's the first and last time I hope to see the backside of a vulture. I don't think I should go on about that. I'm sure you wouldn't want me to. What my husband would do, every morning, he'd take his coffee outside and throw tennis balls at them. You know, buzzards really don't like to be around people."

No wonder. If Chestertown is going to make best advantage of its association with its feathered friends, there's got to be more understanding than comes from thrown balls and banged metal, or they might fly off again to my side of the river where we really don't have the same need for them. If Chestertown is ever going to produce the Winter Buzzard Fest, reaping the benefits that would bring, it's got some things to learn.

As Wayne Bell, former director of the Center for the Environment and Society at Washington College points out, "Basically they're carrion eaters. You'd be up to your rear end in carrion if we didn't have vultures and dung beetles to break it down in a hurry. You don't see dead animals along the roadsides for very long, if you think about it. Thank vultures for it."

It's not easy to love a buzzard, and Bell concedes that. It's going to take commitment. "They have a couple of nasty habits," he observes. "The black vultures defecate down their legs, for one thing.

"It's thought to be for thermal regulation. They don't have leg feathers."

See, a little understanding.

No, vultures aren't birds you'd want to have eating out of your hand. They are, though, just the birds to eat that hand when your circumstances are exactly right. They instinctively know what some humans in Chestertown don't seem to grasp—how to get the most of the feast that is there for the sharing, wherever it is that buzzards and people come together—and how so much, always, depends upon the presentation.

~

Contributors

AFTER A CAREER in the Foreign Service, Sheila Austrian made Kent County her full-time home when she started classes at Washington College in 2001. Majoring in history and a member of ODK, she graduated with the Class of 2003. Sheila is active in Artworks, the Historical Society of Kent County, St. Paul's Church, WC-ALL and local little theater. She lives on a working farm near Chestertown.

Sarah Blackman, who earned a degree from Washington College in 2002, is an MFA student at the University of Alabama where she serves as the fiction editor for the *Black Warrior Review*. Her most recent work appears in *Borderlands, 4am Poetry Review, The Roanoke Review, Touchstone* and the *Best New American Voices, 2006*. She thinks the Black Warrior River is fine and all, but it doesn't hold a candle to the Chester.

John R. Bohrer came to Chestertown in 2002 to study political science and economics. As a New Jersey native who believes curses really do exist, Jack is obviously a Nets basketball fan.

William Chapman Bowie, who graduated from Washington College in 1975, lives in western Massachusetts with his wife and 5 1/2-year-old son.

John Buettner is a 1989 graduate of Washington College and the institution's Director of Media Relations. He has been a railroad enthusiast since his childhood and has often suffered from the "Disappearing American Railroad Blues." He has yet to hobo out of Kent County, though.

Elizabeth C. Clay, from Bethesda, Maryland, is a student at Washington College. A member of the Class of 2008, she plans to major in anthropology and minor in history and French. She enjoys doing primary research especially related to genealogy and the Civil War era.

Robert Day is the founder and past director of the Rose O'Neill Literary House at Washington College, where he is professor of English and American literature, and publisher of The Literary House Press. His novel, *The Last Cattle Drive*, was a Book-of-the-Month-Club Selection. His short fiction has won a number of prizes, including the Seaton Prize, a Pen Faulkner/NEA Prize, and Best American Short Story Citations. His nonfiction has been published in the *Washington Post Sunday Magazine, Smithsonian, Forbes* and *Modern Maturity*. When not in Chestertown, he and his wife, the painter Kathryn Jankus Day, live in St. Michel de Montaigne, France, or Ludell, Kansas.

James Dissette, a 1971 graduate of Washington College, is a newspaper publisher, graphic designer and writer. He lives in northern Michigan but frequently travels back to Chestertown for Literary House Press projects and to see friends and family. A limited edition letterpress book printer, he is working on his next project—seventeen unpublished poems by the 12th century Chinese poet Chin Kuan, translated by William McNaughton, professor emeritus, University of Hong Kong.

Jack Gilden, who earned a degree in the humanities from Washington College in 1987, is president of Gilden Integrated, a marketing, advertising and public relations firm headquartered in Baltimore. He is also an essayist, columnist, literary reviewer, husband and father of two. His credits include *The* Baltimore *Sun, The* Baltimore *Evening Sun, Style Magazine, The Jewish Times, Chesapeake Life, Washington College Magazine, Sports Heritage* and *Rain Taxi*.

Adam Goodheart, the C.V. Starr Scholar at Washington College, writes about history for *National Geographic, The American Scholar, Smithsonian* and other publications; his piece in this book first appeared in somewhat different form in *The American Scholar*. Erin Koster '07, a student in his Spring 2005 course "Chestertown's America" helped with the research for the essay. John R. Bohrer '06, Albin Kowalewski '07, Kees de Mooy '01, and Chris Cerino also contributed valuable information.

Meredith Davies Hadaway's collection of poetry, *Fishing Secrets of the Dead*, was a Word Press First Book Selection in 2005. She serves as Vice President for College Relations and Marketing at Washington College.

P. Trams Hollingsworth, a 1975 graduate of Washington College, served as the school's alumni director for fifteen years. Her son Lenox was raised by the Washington College family and the Chestertown community.

Roy Hoopes, a career political journalist, biographer, historian and author of murder mysteries, is one of America's most prolific freelance writers. He received the Edgar Award *for Cain, The Biography of James M. Cain*, taking as his subject the son of James W. Cain, president of Washington College from 1903 until 1918. Among Hoopes's other works are *When the Stars Went to War: Hollywood and World War II*, and *Our Man in Washington*, a historical novel featuring James M. Cain and H.L. Mencken as detectives. His second novel, *A Watergate Tape*, was published in 2002. Hoopes served as director of public relations at Washington College in the mid-1980s.

Kees de Mooy, a former contractor and father of two current Washington College students, was always fascinated by the history of the buildings he worked on. Chestertown's Sultana Project provided him the impetus to donate his carpenter tools to the effort and to complete his degree in history, graduating summa cum laude in 2001. He has since authored three books; *The Wisdom of John Adams, The Wisdom of Thomas Jefferson*, and *The Wisdom of Abraham Lincoln*. De Mooy is currently the Program Manager at the C.V. Starr Center for the Study of the American Experience.

Jim Landskroener, who earned a master's degree from Washington College in 1991, is a middle school teacher at Kent School in Chestertown. He has been a fond observer of life in Chestertown for almost fifty years, not counting the first few years when he really wasn't old enough to know what was going on. (He found the new brick sidewalks a little pretentious at first and had a real hard time when they took down the overhead traffic lights, but what the heck, no need to be sore about it.) An occasional contributor to the *Washington College Magazine*, he lives close to the college—about a 525-yard par-5 sharp dogleg right, best to hit a 3-wood off the tee—with his fabulous wife, Diane, and two equally fabulous teenage kids, Emmy and Thomas.

Marcia C. Landskroener is director of communications at Washington College. A Rock Hall girl whose ancestral family of shipbuilders and watermen qualifies her as an authentic Eastern Shore native, she is married to Jim's older brother, Chris (see above). She earned a master's degree in English literature from Washington College in 2002.

John Lang is director of the journalism intern program at Washington College. Before moving to the Chestertown area in 2001, he was a writer and editor at The Associated Press, Scripps-Howard News Service, *New York Post, Singapore Straits-Times, U.S. News & World Report* and *The Washington Post*. He came to Chestertown for the waters. He wasn't misinformed.

Andrew R. McCown was born in Chestertown in 1953. Much of his youth was spent on the Chester River, fishing, crabbing and boating. Widely known as Captain Andy, he has been teaching Chesapeake Bay history and ecology with Echo Hill Outdoor School since 1977, when he graduated from Washington College. Happily, the captain still spends a great deal of time on the Chester, sailing the school's 1901 skipjack, the *Elsworth*, out of Chestertown with eager students from all over the Mid-Atlantic region aboard.

Pat Herold Nielsen is a television producer/writer and a founding board member of the Chester River Association. She is the daughter-in-law of the late Lynette Nielsen, in whose name Washington College honors the work of an outstanding student artist each year.

Leslie Prince Raimond, a 1963 graduate, transferred to Washington College from Arizona State College in 1960. She was attracted to the great roots music available all around the area including The Uptown Club and on the radio (WSID out of Baltimore). She has remained a fan ever since. She has worked as a high school English teacher, a ballet instructor and as the activity director at Kent County Senior Center. Currently she is the Executive Director of Kent County Arts Council.

Jean Dixon Sanders is a 1979 graduate of Washington College. Her paintings are in corporate and private art collections. She lives in Sewall's Point, Florida, with her husband and two children. She remembers fondly the beauties of Chestertown and the Eastern Shore. They continue to influence her work.

Bill Thompson has lived on the Eastern Shore from Chestertown to Crisfield for more than thirty-five years, but still considers himself to be an interloper. Aside from childhood excursions to Ocean City, his first meaningful introduction to the Shore came while he was a student at Washington College. He was a weekly newspaper editor in Queen Anne's County and, during part of his eleven years as a reporter for

The (Baltimore) *Sun*, occupied the Eastern Shore Bureau. He has twice worked at his *alma mater*, once in College Relations during Douglass Cater's presidency and later as director of The Literary House Press. He currently resides in Easton.

Nicole Vattimo is a senior at Washington College, where she is pursuing a bachelor of arts degree in English with a focus on journalism. She has come to appreciate Chestertown's long and deep history, and now thinks of it as home.

Kathy Wagner is an assistant professor of English and the Associate Director of the O'Neill Literary House at Washington College, where she earned a degree in 1979. Her work has appeared in *The Midwest Quarterly, Sequoia,* the *Southern Poetry Review,* and most recently in *Weavings 2000, the Maryland Millennial Anthology.* She has been the recipient of a MacDowell Fellowship from the MacDowell Colony for the Arts.

Marshall Williams earned a master's in English at Washington College in 1992, while working as the college's special events coordinator. Marshall went on to earn an M.F.A. in dramaturgy and dramatic literature from the Yale School of Drama. He then worked as Arts and Community Editor for the *Caledonian-Record,* a daily newspaper published in St. Johnsbury, Vermont. In 2003, Marshall moved to Westerly, Rhode Island, to help raise money for the WARM Shelter, a homeless shelter and soup kitchen. He is now Director of Annual Giving at St. Edmund's Retreat at Enders Island in Mystic, Connecticut. Marshall sings and performs with the Chorus of Westerly, and works with the Flock Theatre in New London, Connecticut.

P.J. Wingate, a DuPont executive and vice chair of the College's Board of Visitors and Governors, earned his Washington College degree in 1933. He wrote frequently for the *Washington College Magazine* before his death on May 22, 2000. His essay on Colonel Hiram Brown first appeared in the Spring 1988 edition of the *Washington College Magazine*.

Mary Wood, whose family farm in the wilds of Centreville provided the setting for the James Dickey luncheon, earned a degree in the humanities from Washington College in 1968. A member of the Arts Council in both Kent and Queen Anne's counties, she is one of the founders of the Church Hill Theatre. Her one-act play, *Crossing the Gulf Stream*, won first prize in the Maryland Playwrights Competition. A new play, *Hunting Rights*, will have its world premiere at Church Hill in 2006. She is the author of *My Darling Alice* based on family letters, *The Balanced Moment*, a volume of verse, a children's book and a series of self-published biographies known as *The Grandmother Quartettes*.

Peregrine Wroth (1786-1879) was born on his father's plantation, Town's Relief, just outside Chestertown, and lived in Kent County throughout his long life. After graduating from Washington College in 1803, he became a noted physician, served as professor of chemistry at his alma mater, and published poems and essays on various subjects.

The Editorial Board wishes to thank the Donner Foundation for
providing the funding that made this project possible.

The Board also wishes to recognize the invaluable contributions of
Sarah Snyder for her editorial assistance, Pete Knox for his
man-on-the-street approach to marketing this volume, Bill Ingersoll
for cheerfully answering questions about local history and local
characters, and Tyler Campbell for preserving and recording
images of our past.